Popular Books

By "BRICK" POMEROY.

SENSE—A Book for Hearts and Homes, **$1.50.**

NONSENSE—A Book of Humorous Sketches, **$1.50.**

POMEROY PICTURES OF NEW YORK. [In Press.] **$1.50.**

LIFE OF "BRICK" POMEROY, with Steel Portrait, **$1.50.**

These books are all illustrated, are among the most popular books of the day, are beautifully printed and bound, and will be sent by mail FREE, *on receipt of price,*
BY
**Carleton, Publisher,
New York.**

NONSENSE,

OR

Hits and Criticisms on the Follies of the Day

BY

"BRICK" POMEROY,
(Editor of the La Crosse, Wis., Democrat.)

WITH ILLUSTRATIONS BY J. H. HOWARD.

NEW YORK:
G. W. Carleton & Co., Publishers.
LONDON: S. LOW, SON & CO.
MDCCCLXIX.

Entered according to Act of Congress, in the year 1868, by
G. W. CARLETON & CO.,
In the Clerk's Office of the District Court of the United States for the Southern District of New York.

THE NEW YORK PRINTING COMPANY,
81, 83, *and* 85 *Centre Street*,
NEW YORK.

Dedication.

READER! THIS VOLUME IS DEDICATED TO YOU. IF IT RAISES A SMILE, DRIVES CARE FROM YOUR HEART EVEN FOR AN HOUR, AND MAKES YOU BETTER NATURED,

I am content.

IF YOU CAN WRITE A WORSE BOOK, DON'T DO IT! IF YOU CAN WRITE A BETTER ONE, DO IT QUICKLY FOR THE EDIFICATION OF

"BRICK" POMEROY,

CONTENTS.

CHAPTER	PAGE
I.—Our First Exercise in Skating	11
II.—Science of Kissing	17
III.—Mosquitoes on a Bender	21
IV.—My Milkmaid Miranda	29
V.—My Experience at a New England Sewing-Circle!	33
VI.—Biluria Bulkins and our Courtship	48
VII.—Pickerel-Fishing in Connecticut	56
VIII.—B-o-s-t-o-n-!	63
IX.—How I lost Aurelia	71
X.—The Dog-Gondest Dog	84
XI.—Peter Oleum struck by "Brick."	94
XII.—Teutonic Anguish	104
XIII.—"Brick" and the Deacon's Hexa	109
XIV.—Cure for a Cold	122
XV.—"Brick" Pomeroy sends the President his Ann-Alice	128
XVI.—"Brick" and Kalista	138
XVII.—"Brick" Pomeroy's Evening with Arion	147
XVIII.—"Brick" Pomeroy's Experience at Niagara Falls	155
XIX.—"Brick" Pomeroy Skateth at the Central Park	163
XX.—Boston Betsey's "Brick," or "Brick's" Betsey	176
XXI.—How to Buy Oil Lands	187
XXII.—A Chicken Suit	205
XXIII.—As a Pic-Nic-ist	209
XXIV.—"Brick" and the School-Marms!	219
XXV.—Wisconsin School-Marm Convention	232
XXVI.—The Fun of Sleighing	245
XXVII.—Slobbering Parties—for the Heathen!	254
XXVIII.—Wonderful Hair Reproducer	262
XXIX.—The Dickens	266

AUTHOR'S PREFACE.

IN the first place I did not write this Book.
It was printed.
And the reason I wrote it was simply this:
In 1817 my father owned a large peach-orchard in New Jersey. At the same time he owned a yoke of oxen, and a large covered wagon. The wagon was covered by a shed. A simple shed of excellent habit, inasmuch as it covered the wagon.
At this time my uncle lived in Canada, adjoining the town nearest the one he resided in. He owned a span of horses and a garden. It was a covered garden, covered by weeds.
There was not then, and it is safe to presume there is not now any other resemblance between the wagon of my father and the garden of my uncle, than the fact that each was covered.
Why this was so I never knew, as the nurse left the day beforehand, so I determined to adopt the wisest course, thinking it would be the best. The result was all I wished, and more.
In 1821, the physician moved away, and left the place. My father determined to bind me out as an apprentice to a fine old gentleman whose daughter was in love with a young man who lived with his father down the river which in the spring-time was so swollen by the rains that it was important not to cross it except in a skiff tied to a buttonwood tree by a chain which cost five dollars at the hardware store on the corner of the street in the village where each Sabbath morning the minister told his many congregation which would have been larger had it not been for the habit so many people had of staying away from all places of good instruction without which not a single person in the village would have been safe for a moment from the members of a band of desperadoes whose retreat was in the bowels of a huge mountain, on whose healthy sides

the birds sang all the day long as if to remind the weary passer-by that in all well-regulated families there exists a cause for the effect be it great like the late war which was a fearful struggle on both sides for the original position held by the covered wagon of my father.

Who can wonder at the infatuation of the youth when he saw his own true love in the power of the Indian whose scalping-knife hung suspended from a tree over the grave where a small picket fence had been erected by a boy who saw the fire burst forth devouring in an hour the fruit of a lifetime of toil which unrewarded leaves no recompense to strengthen the soul of man as he wars with evils that beset the path which led to the trysting-tree which had by this time been cut down to make room for a large hotel where the sound of revelry by night was heard booming over the still waters of the lake as the moon shone down upon the sailor-boy stood on a burning deck!

At this moment the breeching gave way and the horse plunged over the precipice, which at this point ran nearly a thousand cubic feet into the cave where the serpent had taken refuge from the coming storm which threatened to burst forth and destroy the entire plan of the temple on which if the workmen had been employed to save the child ere it struck, the bottom of the well down which the bucket descended bringing up the purest ice-water rivalling the alabaster neck of the wounded sufferer whose death happened to plunge the entire city in mourning.

The reader will see at a glance that from this moment, none of us were to blame as the events mentioned will prove.

P.S.—If this preface does not suit, the resignation of the reader will be accepted whenever he visits the sanctum of the author where the following pages were written merely for that

"Little nonsense now and then,
Is relished by the wisest men."

Humorously thine,
"BRICK" POMEROY.

SANCTUM: *La Crosse, Wis.*, 1867.

"Mary said, 'Guess 'taint a handkerchief, Jane,' and Mary was right. It wan't a handkerchief, not a bit of it."
—*Page* 13.

Nonsense.

CHAPTER I.

Our First Exercise in Skating.

RIGHT beneath one of our windows, from morn till midnight, we see youngsters and oldsters twisting their legs into all conceivable shapes, skating up and down the river merry as lambs. We cannot pick up a paper but an article on "skating" meets the eye. Everybody says it's fun, and that's all everybody knows about it, for we've tried it. Last night, about gas-light time, after reading a glowing description of life on skates, we prepared for our first attempt, and sallied forth to join the merry crowd. We had on a pair of stoga boots, trousers-legs tucked inside, a Robert-tailed coat, and white hat. We went down on the ice, and gave a boy two shillings in good coin of the realm for the use of his implements. We have confidence, even as great as Peter's faith. We, with the assistance of a friend, fixed on the skates and stood erect like a barber's pole. Encouraged by the sight of some ladies on the bridge, who were just then looking at the skaters, we struck out. A slant to the right with the right foot, a slant to the left with the left foot, and just then we saw something on the ice and stooped over to pick it up! On our feet again—two slants to the right and one to the left, accompanied with a loss of confidence. Another stride with the right foot, and we sat down with fearful rapidity, and very little if any elegance! What a set-down it was, for we made a dent in the ice not unlike a Connecticut butter-bowl.

Just then one of the ladies remarked, "Oh, look, Mary, that feller with the white hat ain't got his skates on the right place!" Ditto, thought we. Just then a ragged little devil sang out, as he glided past us: "Hallo, old timber legs!" and we arose suddenly and put after him, and away went our legs—one to the east and the other to the west—causing an immense fissure in our pants and another picture of a butter-tray in the cold—*oh, how cold!*—ice! Then the lady again spoke, and said, "Oh, look, Mary, that chap with the white hat has sat down on his handkerchief to keep from taking cold!" We rose about as gracefully as a saw-horse, when Mary said, "Guess 'taint a handkerchief, Jane," and Mary was right. It wan't a handkerchief—not a bit of it. Just then a friend came along and proffered us his coat-tail as a "steadier." We accepted the continuation of his garment, and up the river we went, about ten rods, when a shy to the right by the leader, caused us, the wheel-horse, to scoot off on a tangent, heels up! But the ice is very cold this season!

We tried it again. A glide one way, a glide and a half the other, when whack came our bump of philoprogenitiveness on the ice, and we saw millions of stars dancing around us, like ballet girls at the Bowery Theatre. How that shock went through our system, and up and down our spinal column! Lightning couldn't have corkscrewed it down a greased sapling with greater speed or more exhilarating effect. Boarding-house butter nor warranty deed could have struck any stronger than we did—and a dozen ladies looking at us and our fissured pants!

"Hallo, old cock!" sang out that ragged imp again, and we there helpless. Soon we got up and made another trial with better success. Perhaps we had skated, in our peculiar style, fifteen feet, when a blundering chap came up behind,

Our First Exercise in Skating.

and we sat down, with our tired head pillowed in his lap, and he swearing at us, when it was all his fault! How cold the ice was there, too! Every spot where we made our *début* on the ice, oh, how cold it was! Our nice bear-skin was no protection at all. We tried again, for the papers all say it's fun, and down came our Roman-Grecian nose on the cold julep material, and the little drops of crimson ran down our shirt-bosom, and on to the cold ice!

Once more we tried skating—made for the shore—sat down and counted damages. Two shillings in cash thrown away; seven lateral and one "fronternal" bumps on the ice; one immense fissure in as handsome a pair of ten-dollar cassimeres as a man ever put his legs in; one rupture in the knee, extending to the bone; four buttons from our vest; a fragmented watch-crystal, and a back-ache big enough to divide among the children of Israel! If you catch us on the smooth, glassy, chilling, freezing, treacherous, deceitful, slippery, and slip-uppery ice again, you'll know it! If any one ever hears of our skating again, they will please draw on us at sight for the bivalves and accompanying documents. We have got through. It's a humbug! It's a vexation of spirit, of business, of flesh, and tearer of trousers! It's a head-bumping, back-aching, leg-wearying institution, and we warn people against skating. We tried it, and shan't be able to walk for a month. Skating clubs are humbugs, and the only reason why the rascally youngsters wish to get the ladies at it, is that they may see—if they, too, don't say "the ice is dreadfully cold!" It's nothing to us, it's nothing to us; but the ladies will do as well to let skates alone, unless they are younger and more elastic than are we! Oh, how cold the ice is—we can feel it yet!

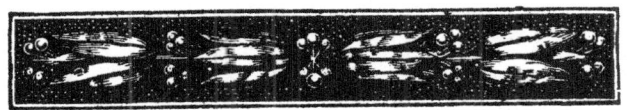

CHAPTER II.

SCIENCE OF KISSING.

PEOPLE will kiss, yet not one in a hundred knows how to extract bliss from lovely lips, no more than they know how to make diamonds from charcoal. And yet it is easy—at least for us! This little item is not alone for young beginners, but for the many who go at kissing like hunting coons or shelling corn.

First, know who you are to kiss. Don't make a mistake, although a miss take may be good. Don't jump up like a trout for a fly, and smack a woman on the neck, the ear, one corner of her forehead, the end of the nose, or slop-over on her waterfall or bonnet-ribbon, in your haste to get through.

When God made the world He went slow, and at last pronounced it "very good." Ditto kissing. And morning and night were the first day! It is simple, yet excellent. The gent should be a little the tallest. He should have a clean face, a kind eye, a mouth full of expression, instead of tobacco. Don't kiss all over, as grasshoppers walk. Don't kiss everybody, including nasty little dogs, male or female. Don't sit down to it. Stand up. You need not be anxious to get in a crowd. Two persons are plenty to corner and catch a kiss! More persons spoil the sport! Stand firm. It won't hurt after you are used to it!

Take the left hand of the lady in your right hand. Let your hat go to—any place out of the way! Throw the left hand gently over the shoulder of the lady, and let the hand fall down upon her right side, toward the belt. Don't be

Science of Kissing. 19

in a hurry! Draw her gently, lovingly, to your heart. Her head will fall lightly upon your shoulder — and a handsome shoulder-strap it makes! Don't be in a hurry! Send a little life down your left arm, and let it know its business. Her left hand is in your right. Let there be expression to your grasp—not like the grip of a vice, but a gentle clasp, full of electricity, thought, and respect. Don't be in a hurry!

Her head lies carelessly on your shoulder! You are nearly heart to heart! Look down into her half-closed eyes! Gently yet manfully press her to your bosom! Stand firm, and Providence will give you strength for the ordeal! Be brave, but don't be in a hurry!

Her lips almost open! Lean lightly forward with your head—not the body. Take good aim —the lips meet—the eyes close—the heart opens —the soul rides the storms, troubles, and sorrows of life (don't be in a hurry)—heaven opens before you—the world shoots from under your feet as a meteor flashes athwart the evening sky (don't be afraid)—the nerves dance before the just-erected altar of love as zephyrs dance with the dew-trimmed flowers—the heart forgets its bitterness, and the art of kissing is learned! No noise—no fuss—no fluttering and squirming, like hook-impaled worm.

Kissing don't hurt—does not require a brass band to make it legal. Don't jab down on a beautiful mouth as if spearing for frogs! Don't grab and yank the lady, as if she was a struggling colt! Don't muss her hair—scrunch down her collar—bite her cheeks—squizzle her rich ribbons, and leave her mussed, rumpled, and mum-muxed! Don't flavor your kisses with onions, tobacco, gin cocktails, lager-beer, brandy, etc., for a maudlin kiss is worse than —— to a delicate, loving, sensitive woman. Try the above recipe, and, if you do not succeed, for further particulars call on, or write to " BRICK " POMEROY.

CHAPTER III.

Mosquitoes on a Bender.

NIGHT before last, in order to sleep, we placed a piece of raw beefsteak on a plate at the head of our bed. In the morning it was by the mosquitoes sucked as dry of blood as an old sponge, and our skin saved at least two thousand perforations. All about the room, in the morning, were mosquitoes, plethoric with blood, loaded till they could not fly. We killed a few, but the job was too sanguinary, so we left them to their feast.

Last night, in order to get even with the serenading devils, we steeped half a pound of fresh beefsteak in some old rye whiskey, and left it on a plate by the bed. Nothing like being hospitably inclined. In ten minutes after the light was extinguished, a swarm of these backbiting billposters made an advance movement. One of them caressed us sweetly on the nose—he sent in his bill—there was a slap—a diluted damn—a dead mosquito! Soon we heard a tremendous buzzing about the whiskey-soaked beef. The entire mosquito family came singing in, and such an opera—good Lord deliver us! But they did not disturb us with bites. We fell asleep, to be awakened in ten minutes by the worst mosquito-concert ever editor, mortal, devil, angel, divine, Dutchman, or any other man listened to. We raised a light, and the greatest show of the season was there to be seen. Every mosquito was drunk as a blind fiddler, and such an uproarious night as the long-billed whelps had, never was seen before this side of—*selah!* The worst antics! Some were playing circus on the plate.

One big fellow, with a belly like Falstaff, full of blood and whiskey, was dancing juba on the Bible, while a fat friend of his lay on her back beating the devil's dream on an invisible tambourine, with one hind leg! Two more were wrestling on the foot-board of the bedstead, each with his bill stuck fast in the timber. Another was tying the legs of our pants into a bow-knot to fasten about the neck of Anna Dickinson—whose picture hangs against the washstand—while another red-stomached customer was trying to stand on his head in the wash-bowl.

All over the room were drunken mosquitoes! One long-billed, gaunt representative, was trying to ram the mucilage bottle full of newspaper clippings. Another chap was drilling a hole through a revolver handle, and singing "My Mary Ann;" while still another was limping across the window-sill in search of fresh air, to the agonizing tune of "Tramp, tramp, tramp!" One little rat of a skeet was trying to jam the cock out of Ben. Butler's eye with a tooth-brush, as his picture hung in the room beside that of Kidd, the pirate. A drunken statesman of the mosquito family was talking Russian to a lot of drunken companions, as they lay in a heap on the plate, while another one sat in the handle of our bowie-knife, doubled up with cramp in the stomach, and trying to untie his tail with his bill, which seemed like Lincoln's backbone when Anna Dickinson said it wanted stiffening. He was a sick-looking skeeter, and died in three minutes after we saw him, her, or it, as the case may be. Two others took a bath in the inkstand. One, with a bill like the devil's narrative, was trying to wind our watch with a pen-wiper, while another died as he was sitting on the rim of a dish in the room, trying to chaunt "Mother, I've come home to die!" Poor skeeter. A nice skeeter, but "'twas a pity he drank." An old veteran, with a paunch full of 'alf and 'alf—blood and whiskey—sat on the table, reading Les

Mosquitoes on a Bender.

Misérables, while his wife was under the stove trying to mend her broken wing with a limpsey toothpick. She looked disgusted! Another one combed his hair with a paper of pins, tied a piece of white paper about his neck, pasted a five-cent infernal revenue stamp on his rump—or words to that effect—and died like a "loyal" citizen. His last words were—

"Tell the traitors all around you," etc., etc.

Another drunken scamp started out of the window for John B. Gough, or a stomach-pump. A worse behaved set of bummers we never saw. They acted fearfully. About two thousand lay around dead, but sadness seemed not to break in upon their hilarious rioting upon blood and whiskey. Half-a-dozen of them sat on our new hat playing draw-poker, using worm lozenges for checks, while one of the party got clean busted by making a fifty-dollar blind good on a four-flush, which didn't fill! He will be apt to wear cotton socks next winter, and keep away from church collection days. Another one sat on top of a brandy bottle, reading "Baxter's Call to the Unconverted," while his partner lay dead at his feet, evidently forced to close doors by the failure of Ketchum & Son, of New York! Six others were trying to hang one that looked like a Copperhead, to the corner of a match-safe; but as they were drunk and he sober, it was not safe to bet on his being dangled. They ate the beef, drank the blood and whiskey, drilled the plate full of holes, and on the centre-table organized a Son of Malta lodge, using a five-cent shin-plaster for blanket in the act entitled "The Elevation of Man."

Another red-bellied leader of the Miss Keeter family had a battalion of drunken bummers on the edge of a spittoon watching him jam a fur overcoat into his left ear. He acted foolish— foolish enough for a brigadier-general or member of congress. A little cuss with black legs, crimson stomach, and double-jointed bill, was vomiting in a satin slipper, while his wife, a sickly-looking lady of her tribe, was gnawing at the bed-post, thinking it a bologna. Another one, evidently an old maid, sat under the sofa milking the cat, while her sister was crowding a pair of woollen drawers into her waterfall, singing in a subdued strain—

"Come rest in this bosom!"

We have applied for a season ticket—front seat.

Another one, with a certificate of marriage over his head in the shape of a welt the size of a candle-mould, was dancing a fandango with two mosquito virgins on a watch-crystal, while a deacon in one of their churches sat playing old sledge with a corkscrew, to see which should go for a gin cocktail. An artistic delegate was standing on his head in a champagne tumbler, one hind leg run through his under jaw, while with the other he was pointing out the road to Richmond to a lot of skeets still drunker than himself, who were sitting dog-fashion on the pillow. We should say it was a gay party—quitely so!

Talk about shows, concerts, dog-fights, amputations, circuses, negro funerals, draw-poker, sparking, or other amusements, there is nothing to be compared to a flock of mosquitoes on a bender. If you don't believe it, fix them up with a piece of beefsteak soaked in whiskey, and laugh your sides sore at the antics the drunken warblers cut.

CHAPTER IV.

My Milkmaid Miranda.

I LOVED a milkmaid, Miranda by cognomen, and she was the quickest milkist that ever squatted garter-holders under the dripping eaves of a patient bovine on a day of rain, and sich. She was handsome. Her mother was a handsome cuss, and her father was a blessing in disguise, with mien like an angel and hair colored like a New Jersey barn.

Miranda lived in New England. Her paternal pap engineered a country store, kept blooded geese, sold potatoes by the pound, kept cheese rinds for rat-trap bait, blackened pins and sold them for fish-hooks, furnished steam for a Puritan prayer-meeting, cultivated a duck pond, and taught his nose to blush on apple brandy. He'd take the screws out of his mother's coffin and sell them for money to put on the church contribution-plate, and he never missed attending communion in order to get a free lunch at the expense of—never mind who!

But Miranda wan't like him. She milked the cows and strained the milk. I used to help her. We were both boys—that is, I was a boy, then. I was green, but pure. Ditto Miran. She was tall. She was long for this world. She was fat as a toothpick. She had a neck like a bottle of Worcester sauce. She was slim as the salary of a country minister, or the wardrobe of a country editor washing-day. And didn't I sling love into her lap? You bet! And didn't she sling milk into her little twelve-quart tin pail, while I used to stand and hold the drooping backbone con-

My Milkmaid Miranda. 31

tinuation of that bovine cow, lest it soil the tinted cheek of my milkmaid, Miranda?

We loved. How could we help it? Her mother was opposed to the match. She thought Miranda wan't good enough for me. I had the poverty. It struck in before I struck out. Being poor, I was good; hence the objection. So we courted syruptastingly, and met in the barnyard the usual way—through the back gate. Every night I veni'd and vidi'd. Her mother used to catch us at it. She enticed Miranda into bedrooms, cellars, pantries, and closets, and there confined her before her time came for going out to milk.

But we often circumvented the aged matron. We changed clothes with the hired man, and went in on our nerve. Miranda loved. "Brick" loved. But we had hard times of it. Affection gurgles as it runs. Our affection ran not smoothly. The darned thing won't run smooth Selah!

We used to wander after beech-nuts, and the old lady was there. We sallied forth to gather shells of ocean—as we called hen's eggs—in the hay-mow, and behold! the old lady was there. We went forth hand in hand, like the ghost of John Brown and that other man, in search of a love-lit bower, and behold! there appeared the aged who first knew Miranda, and bade us return. She was an agile mother. We sat under the window to compare our tales of love, and Miranda's mother inflicted shower-baths upon us the while. We attended funerals in order to have fun, but behold she was there, and our fun came not to pass. At times I rode the family horse by the window at stated periods when Miranda was to be there, and the voice of my milkmaid's maternal was always saying, "Let's see how fast you dare ride!" She locked up the barn-door to keep us from entering therein. She locked up the parlor to keep us from courting there. She stuck sticks over the kitchen door latch to keep us out of that apartment. She locked Miranda up in a cellar to keep us from descending into that damp place. I said in my puny wrath, "Dog-gone that ancient female!" I had but one hand to love Miranda with—the other was needed to battle the second volume of Miranda's authorship with. My love sank. It lowered. It prostrated. I went to Canada. I remained in the embrace of the Queen, as 'twere After a time the old lady, at the close of a delightful trip of nine weeks' duration, arrived at the grave-yard, thanks to a doctor, whose doctorin I ever recommended in such cases. The little posy-rosy, the hollyhock, and the asparagus bloomed over the maternal derivative of my milkmaid, and made me happy. I shouted in unison with merry roosters and the vernal chickens, and sought her I loved. Twelve years had gone and done it. But Miranda stuck it out. No one could look upon the face of her ma, and survive. I was the exception. Miranda's father had passed in his checks. He grew tired of life, and after a fit of family happiness took the poison the rats refused, and went joyfully from the arms of Miranda's maternal mother to death, and its results, as 'twere.

Miranda had the things she inherited, such as geese, the little store, the cheese rinds, the warbling ducks, and all sich of the estate, and threw open the shutters of her heart. I popped in. The front room thereof was vacant. I slung in my traps, crawled in at the window, took possession, sang a song of joy, kissed my milkmaid on her dinner-catcher, sold my disappointment for a yellow necktie, and became an altered man, full of joy where sorrow had so lately nestled. We courted. We wedlocked. We sold the old homestead. We went to *B—o-s-thn* (with the "thn" up your nose), and went in for style!

There was a party. Miranda fixed up for it. Miranda was flush from the proceeds of the homestead. She bought a cow's worth of frizzled hair, a sheep's worth of lace for her garters, a hog's worth of night blushing seriousness, and the earnings of the geese, bees, chickens and ducks her father had for years, and went to the ball. But she was gay! Hardly knew her. She looked large. Such a bust! Such colors! Such teeth! Such hair! Such complexion! Such palpitators! Such poached front hair, and such scrambled back hair! She was raised in Weathersfield, New England, and was weaned on onions. I knew her by her gentle breath. But for this I would have lost her.

We wore out the party. All fashionable people stay to extinguish the lamps. Style. We went home. There was a cry of fire. Our house was in flames. Miranda had gone to her retirary while I was writing a description of the party. I heard the alarm. I rushed into our bedroom. I found something slim and docile in the bed! I thought it was the bolster got the wrong way.

My Milkmaid Miranda.

I wanted to act in fireman style, so threw a mirror out of the window to let the crowd down-stairs know all was safe above; then ran down with bolster in my arms. This long slim bolster was Miranda, my milkmaid! She had decreased. Affected by fear. I sat her down under the parlor window, in a rose-bush, that the crowd might not see "the charms her downcast modesty," etc., failed to conceal.

Then I ran back to get her things, spread in five chairs at the foot of the bed and lying in circles on the floor. I got them. Nine armsful when I had them all. The house was in ruins, and Miranda was burned to death. I felt bad! Who could help it? Pardon my weakness, but I wept. Yet I was consoled. Though gone, she was with me still. I had all that made her lovely. I had her curls, her frizzle, her rats, her waterfall! I had her spiral palpitators, her bird's-nest, her veals! I had a set of teeth, a steel compress for the ankles! I have set all things in their order. I have them hung on wires. I shall pour a little melted girl (easy to be had this hot weather) into the fixings, and have an udder Miranda. How lucky to save so much of her!

Ever of theely,
"Brick" Pomeroy.

CHAPTER V.

My Experience at a New England Sewing-Circle!

"The Christian ladies of this congregation are invited to meet, Thursday evening, at the residence of Mrs. Sniveller, to form a Sewing-Society. A full attendance is requested."

SUCH, my dear hearers, reads a notice I find on my sacred desk this morning, and I read it in hopes you will profit thereby.

We will now sing Psalm cxxxi., first two stanzas:

A New England Sewing-Circle. 39

  My heart not haughty is, O Lord,
   Mine eyes not loftly be;
  Nor do I deal in matters great,
   Or things too high for me!

  I surely have myself behav'd
   With spirit great and mild
  As child of mother weaned; my soul
   Is like a weaned child.

All sing!

Says I, "Bully." Not in a bully spirit, but with a sort of Puritanical meaning, and concluded to go. Mrs. Sniveller — Mrs. Deacon Sniveller — lived in a large white house, in a stone-patch under the hill, down by her husband's button shop. Mrs. Sniveller was a leading horse, so-called, in the team of benevolence at Buttonville. She had a little peaked red nose, about right to open clams with; a nervous jerk to her head, spiral enticers, and a waterfall the size of a plum-pudding, but filled with more ingredients. Deacon Sniveller passed the plate Sabbaths, and took the funds home to count. Mrs. Sniveller always gave with great liberality on the next Sunday!

I wanted to go. I borrowed hoops, skirts, waterfalls, and etceteras. I puffed my front-hair, slung my waterfall on my bump of obstinacy, hoisted an onion into the reticule I carried on the left arm, shouldered a green cotton umbrella, took a piece of red flannel to make a shirt for some little innocent bud on the tree of Abolitionism, and sallied forth, as the Yankee clock struck two.

Mrs. Sniveller was in. The front parlor and the middle parlor was full of noble women, while the best bedroom was full of bonnets, green umbrellas, and reticules, in which to carry home sweetcakes, tarts, biscuit, plum pits, apple cores, and such little things slyly slipped from Mrs. Sniveller's table.

Mrs. Sniveller didn't know me. I told her I was little Sally Squiggle, as what lived there

"Lordy massy, so it is! Why how natural you do look! Bless me, let me kiss my dear Sally."—*Page* 41.

ten years before, and had been South teachin' skule!

"Lordy massy, so it is! Why, how natural you do look, now it all comes to me agin? Bless me! let me kiss my dear Sally, who has escaped from the wretches!" And angelic Mrs. Sniveller came near putting my right eye *hors de combat* with the end of her nose!

I was introduced. Nineteen women were glad to see me, and kissed their dear little Sally till my waterfall got skewed clear around under my left ear, and I began to feel a rising sensation in my throat from the hugging then and there given—or words to that effect.

After I had been so affectionately gone through, I went into the bedroom to reconstruct! Gracious! My waterfall had got under my left ear, making me look as if some ugly man of sin had lifted me one with brass knuckles, and forgot to take it home with him, while my beautiful front hair resembled a garden full of pea-vines after a hurricane. But I retained my composure, and went out to become the centre of attraction.

"My dear Sally!"

"Precious Sally!"

"Little Sally Squiggle, sure enough!"

"So glad you cum hum!"

"Neow dew tell us all abeout it!"

Mrs. Sniveller was made chairman, and the following resolutions were adopted:

"*Resolved*, That this shall be called the Buttonville Benevolent Baby Association.

"*Resolved*, That Mrs. Sniveller be, and hereby are, our President.

"*Resolved*, That our aim is to help the downtrodden and bedridden daughters of Ham, now in the clutches of that vile people, and to this end every member of the B. B. B. make one little flannel shirt a week, and Sally Squiggle shall tell us the size.

"*Resolved*, That we open and close our Society with prayer.

A New England Sewing-Circle.   43

"*Resolved*, That each one of the members invite some man to go home with her at night." (Here I was about to object for fear of exposure, but for fear of exposure I didn't object.—*Sally*.)

After the Society was organized, I was kept so busy answering questions that I came near not finishing the baby envelope I was working on, and should not, had I not took long stitches, as people do in benevolent sewing!

Mrs. Sniveller said:

"Now, Sally, ain't that ere Southern people the hatefullest proud people the world ever did see? Cousin John, who went down as a sutler, brought home two trunks of the proudest silks, laces, jewelry that was real gold, and set with purty stones that was real diamonds, and worth a power of money. He found them in bureaus, trunks, closets, and sich places. The sneaking, coward-men, had gone off to kill our good people, and the women were at work in the hospitals, and all John had to do was to whip a lot of little children and help himself! I know them ere folks are a wicked, mean, ongrateful set, and ought to be killed."

Mrs. Puritan wanted to know if it was true that the people of the South actually cooked biled dinners on Sunday? If they did, she really hoped her cousin in Congress would pass a law that whenever a man in the South cooked a biled dinner on Sunday, he should be hung before dinner, and his biled dinner should be sent North!

Mrs. Pinchbeck hoped the war would continner to go on till there was no more end of nothing. For her part, it was all stuff about the people suffering during the war. Her Josiah had a contract, and made two hundred thousand dollars the first year; and when her brother, Rev. Peaknose Ranter, came back from the war—where he had periled his precious life eating preserves so they would not hurt sick soldier—she brought home more than fifty gold watches, and the nicest gold-clasp Bible, which was now used every Sunday in one of the Buttonville churches.

Mrs. Squeak said the people of the South were nothing but murderers; for when her brother, Colonel Fibre Hunter, was out in a field, doin' nothin', killin' nobody, doin' nothin' but just seein' how much cotton an army team could draw, so he could tell if it was a good team, some cowardly gorilla shot a hole clean through him, and wouldn't even send his clothes home for her Jedediah to wear out! And she hoped if another war ever did come, some of them sinful men of the West would go down and do it to 'em agin; not that she cared so much for her brother, but she wanted them are clothes for her Jedediah!

Mrs. Cockeye said she hoped there would be a hull passel of wars; for her cousin, her dear good cousin, Benjamin (the Beast), had made lots of money in the late war, and had supplied nearly all her relatives with spoons, watches, silverware, etc.; and said it was right the war should go on, for her cousin was safer in war than before a court of justice, even; and said it was a Christian duty to let all Christian wars be continnered so long as there was anybody to continner 'em.

Mrs. Sniveller here spoke again:

"Well, I don't care, nohow. The South should be fought! What right had they to have cotton picked by niggers without asking our consent? And they were rich. And they had nice things. And we believe a nigger baby is of more account than a white pauper in the North. And my husband, Deacon Sniveller, wants more bones to make buttons of; he'll sell the buttons to the South and West, and they will have to pay us New England Christians for the privilege of wearing out their own bones."

By this time tea was ready. We had a good tea. Such curious silver-ware — old-style, pure silver—didn't taste brassy a bit, and all of us ladies tasted all the silver dishes to see! And such a lot of spoons! Each one of us had at our plate a spoon with our initials on. Mrs. Snivéller had a barrel of silver spoons, and hunted them over till she found our regular initials in regular order! Oh, it was so nice! And we piled all the shirts up in a chair, and put a Bible, rescued from the wicked South, on the top of the pile, and then Rev. Mr. Slammer came in and made a prayer, while Mrs. Drawler, on a nice rosewood piano, played that patriotic piece of music—

"John Brown's body lies mouldering in the grave!
John Brown's body lies mouldering in the grave!
John Brown's body lies mouldering in the grave!
Glory, Glory, Hallelujah!"

After which the Buttonville B. B. Society of Buttonville, Commonwealth of Massachusetts, adjourned till next Thursday, when I am going again, if they don't find out that Sally Squiggles is
That horrid
"BRICK" POMEROY.

CHAPTER VI.

Biluria Bulkins and our Courtship.

BILURIA was a husky Seraphim, descended all O. K. from ancient Bulkins, who used to sit on a mackerel tub in Deacon Whezeener's grocery, with his legs crossed, and tell what a powerful delegate he was when he was a young man. He was the man. He was the individual as what had the sylph I sparked. Biluria was his dart. And a nice darter she were. She had a mother—a nice lump of lean, who wore a peaked nose, a pair of black stockings, knit springy at the top to save garters, and for twenty-five years went about the house before going to bed, clad like an angel, with a fire-shovel in one hand and a tallow-dip in the other, looking to see as how as if that ere dod-derned cat had concluded to stay in or to go out. I don't like cats, except in fiddle-strings. Mrs. Bulkins was a vehement catist—she always had more cats than doughnuts in the house. Biluria didn't hanker after cats, but then could endure them. There was one cat—Mr. T. Cat. He was a handsome and a feline rascal. He devastated milk-pans, and created funerals in hen-coops about young chicken time, and made a telescope of his tail every moonlight night on the roof of the woodshed, accompanied by more cat and much yell. He was the only feline Biluria could endure. Gushing Biluria! She used to sit up nights when I went to spark her, with that blessed c-a-t in her lap, right where my head ought to be, and pull its little slender whiskers. Said I: "Biluria, do so by me!" Said Biluria: "Oh, your wiskers ain't big enough to pull, yet." Then we'd eat a doughnut, and drink some cider, and look in the fire. Then I'd listen to the snoring of the two Bulkinses in the setting-room bedroom, and Biluria would sit and play with the cat's tail. Said I: "Biluria, do so!" No, I didn't say so, neither; I just said: "Biluria, if you don't diminish those cat on them floor, I'll occupy them lips for a kiss!" And down always went the cat, and I occupied Biluria, so to speak, and kissing was thus enjoyed. "*Twas nice!*" It weakens me now to think of it. To turn one of Biluria's kisses over in the store-room of memory is no fool of a job. Biluria had red lips, and the sweetest ever investigated. I used to investigate them. I was the committee to do that are. My arms were my credentials. I used to hold out my credentials. Skirmish to the front, throw out my pickets, rally to the breastworks of affection, tie my credentials about Biluria's breadbasket, and go in radically for a lover's kiss.

Oh! I guess not! Biluria was the sweetest kisser in the world, except when she'd been eating onions. She was a Wethersfield girl—a Connecticut child of sorrow—and oft did fill her pancake-trap with onions. At those times the nectar of love was a little strong—too strong to gush much. But at other times 'twas no use talking. Why, one of her kisses would last me a week, if I couldn't get more! They used to gush out all over, run down my shirt bosom into my vest pocket, and solidify like candy. I used to bite them off, there, as from little sticks of candy.

I could not always be with Biluria. I had the wood to cut, the cows to fodder, the sheep to corn, the hens to roost, the swine to feast, the steers to chase away from the wheat-stack, and the apples to sort, and this kept me from Biluria. But while I was hence from her, she made up kisses, ripened them on her lips, and left them hanging there for me to pluck. And you bet I was a lively pluckist on those occasions.

One time old Bulkins was took. He was a deacon. He made prayers at night over two hours, long, and he wan't a stuttering man, either! I was there. Biluria was there. The old lady Bulkins was there, asleep. Biluria took hold of my hand with her hand, and we went to sleep. We thus reposed nigh onto two hours. At last Bulkins terminated! He had consoled the old lady to slumber, and reposed Biluria and I. He was thunder-struck quitely when he came to. He was naturally a jokist, so from a warm room he entered into the outer air for an icicle to gently touch the old lady and Biluria where my "love lies dreaming." The cold comfort he brought in wakened us, but in going out for it he caught cold. The next day he wheezed a little. I wanted to try heave medicine, but he wouldn't. I saw he was took. He saw it. We all felt bad, for the old Bulkins was rich, and it is hard for the rich to die! The old lady found comfort in a black bottle. She was a gin-uine spiritualist! Biluria and I found consolation, too. She had lots of it—enough for me, at all events!

The old man lingered. He was saving. He didn't want to die in the winter, for it was more expensive to open the earth, then. He was near-sighted, but at last he saw something. He remarked but little. He said, perhaps we had better wed. He was facetious, even in his agony. He said: "My two B.'s, if it must B so, let it B so, though I don't see how it can be. Send for a minister, and a mature almanac." Bulkins left soon after. We marched forth with him in March. Mrs. Bulkins lingered and went also. We inserted her by the side of the other Bulkins. One night I felt a little thick, and went to the buttery for the gin bottle! It was empty! Who wouldn't die when the bottle refused to respond?

"I would not live always,
  I would not if I could;
  So I slung the empty bottle,
  And put another where it stood!"

And thus I inherited Biluria, and the farm, and the stock, and the old wagons, and the fences, and the potato holes, and the trash in the barn, and the broad acres of Bulkins, the parient of Biluria. It's a good way to amass wealth. Better than working for it, and more nicer. And now you ought to see us. We go to church every Sunday. We have nigh onto twenty little Bilurias and "Bricks," and there is no good reason why, in course of time, we may not have a family to rise up in the morning and quarrel about their shoes and stockings, till their blessed mother gives them all a warm spot to sit down on. We hope, and more too. I am happy now. We never read newspapers, for that would be a waste of money. We just go along on the road of life, at a jig-jog gait, and nothing troubles us.

I'm a sort of easy delegate. Biluria is the only literary one in the family. She don't care much to read papers winter nights, but is death on old almanacs and such, and I am a happy

"Brick" Pomeroy.

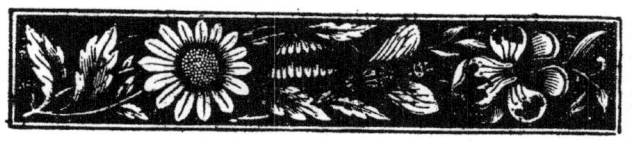

CHAPTER VII.

PICKEREL-FISHING IN CONNECTICUT.

CHRISTMAS and Sunday made a joint-stock concern this year, and skirmished in together. We saw them approach, and retired in good order, so as not to embarrass them during their "toflight" hours. Very considerate, of course! Christmas and Sunday went out together. We fear for Sunday, as Christmas is a hilarious chap, in honor of whose birth all who have the stamps get high. Selah!

Buck and we took much second dinner with Holcomb, ye uproarious, whose residence, on the elevation, towers far above the other towers.

Pickerel-Fishing in Connecticut.

Then we advanced on two bodies of the enemy, well entrenched. We advanced rapidly, and went home before Christmas and Sunday dissolved their joint-stock concern.

And in the morning we awoke. Hair felt heavy. So young, and yet so fair! So light, and yet no lightning. Buck said pickerel-fishing would cure the hair. S'pose Buck knows. Who knows?

Advanced out of bed in good order. Flanked a liberal breakfast. Struck ile on our boots. Boy skirmished on a hardware store, and returned with much fish-lines and large majorities of pickerel-hooks. We took our pick. Went for mummy-chubs. Nice bait, those mummy-chubs. Fat little fellows from the salt sea foam, with much wiggle. Captured many of those—at least seven hundred. Very moist out. Rain was on the fall muchly. Made for Factory Pond. Buck carried two field-pieces, loaded. We carried mummy-chubs. Got to pond. Nice pond, with ice on its cold bosom. Nice rain, but a little too wet. Forgot the hooks. Sent boy two miles to the rear for hooks, which came up in good order. Cut numerous holes through the ice—like perforating for petroleum. Married the hook to the wiggler mummy-chub, and dropped a line to the pickerel. Sat down on the ice to wait for a bite. Patience is a good thing—very good thing. Saw Buck balancing a columbiad on his chin. We skirmished down upon him in time to turn in for relief! Thought it was "inducing" to the pickerel. Borrowed one of Buck's *inducers*, and fell back to original position. Very fine rain in Bridgeport. Lots of holes in the cerulean skimmer. Confound the pickerel. We induced them in vain. Weather quite perspiring. Buck gave up in despair. We maintained, baited anew, and induced every four minutes. Very fine fishing in Factory Pond. Rather too fine. How easy it rained upon the just as well as the unjust. It was a pickerel or two bottles of wine. So we kept inducing, but in vain. At last the glass columbiad ceased to chipper! How natural it is to mourn for departed spirits. Selah! Not another drop—as the man said after he was hung. The rain fell through, but who cares? The little fat wiggling mummy-chubs floated in the tin pail—a pail full of triumphant glee of most of fish's character. But not a pickerel. Four long hours sitting on the cold dampness. It was worse nor sparking. Nary a bite, nary a pickerel; but one sucker was taken in!

We returned in good order. Got home at four o'clock, hungry and dry—considering the weather. Buck wanted the wine—we had it. Went to room. Felt chilly. Raw air is rasping on fine blood. Drew table beside hot coal stove. Drew chair up to table. Pulled a wooden thing hitched to a wire. Thought it was a fish-line! Was fun, so we pulled again. Man came up. Went down. Came again. Left a glass swan,

with long neck but with good body. Hot water and lumps of sugar. The house grew quiet. * *
It grows quieter. The fluid evaporeth from the transparent prison. The bell-rope dances a jig—mummy-chub at other end of it! Very fine weather. Warm weather. Boots come off hard. Some fellow's head feels buzzy. Hair aches. The ink-stand ain't on the stand—it won't stand still two consecutive seconds. Four holes in that ink-stand. The pen has split itself into two pens. The lines on this paper run to skirmish with each other. The lamp looks like a new moon. The stove danceth a jig to invisible music. Fine day for spirits. Big day for pickerel. Good pickerel—no danger fishing for 'em—*they won't bite anybody!* Honest pickereler! Wouldn't *hook* one for the world. Darned pen is sick. Tried to *induce* it to write. Used up all the rye cider inducing. Good pen— fine holder, but can't hold-er steady. Nice place to fish in is Factory Pond. Can fish there all

Pickerel-Fishing in Connecticut. 61

day, just as easy! We see lots of fish now. Sea eels in our boots. Nice eels, but very lively. Nice boots, with '*eels* on 'em. The eminent chanticleer who ruled this paper must have been cross-eyed, for hang us if the parallels run straight. One more enemy in those glass concern. It concerns us. Spirited enemy. Come rest in this chest! It resteth muchly. Hurrah for pickerel! New England pickerel! They must have been on a bust to-day. How small the bottles are since this cruel war is over, no Irish need apply. Wish those bell rope would waltz up this way. Would go and yank it, but don't feel well. Then, we are no Yankee. Tried to reach it. Can't do it. Nice bell rope. Little too wild for steady use. Nice country for game, when rats run up a man's limbs, and eels crawl in his boots for the rest—the rest, ze rest— z'rest! Wonder of z'sem pickerelzes ever bite za'selves? Mus' be, for za won't bite us, an we *induced* z'sem with muchness. Three cheers for fi—fi any man—any Dick-er-in-son or any other man. "Darn z'at bell-rope—it ain't in z'e right posi—po—pozizhun! Connecticut fisherel picking z'ra umburg an' z'o zot bell er' ope!

CHAPTER VIII.

B-o-s-t-o-n-!

BOSTON is the cradle of Lib! The place where Mr. Warren fell and hurt himself. The place where Wendell Phillips, the "silver-tongued" orator, doth abide. It is the "hub of the universe," and the dwelling-place of the big organ. Boston thinks she is the largest place in this world—or the next. Boston is a very complacent burg. We rather like Boston, for there is no village like unto it, from the fiddling of Nero to the Revelation of St. John, N. B.!

Half way between Providence and Boston—

for Boston is a long ways from *Providence*—as we were riding in a car, a still small voice, like the whistle of an engine, broke upon the air. A gentleman in the seat with us uncovered his bald head, and, with a smile, bade us listen!
"What's that?" said we.
"The big organ in Boston!" said he, with a funeralic wave of his hand.
"The devil!" said we.
"Thou shalt not profane!" said the spokesman from the hub.
"Hast been to Boston?" asked he of the silver tongue.
"We hast notist," replied we, then there to him.
He looked—"poor heathen!" He said we must visit the Cradle of Liberty. We asked him if Fred Douglass and Anna Dickinson had engaged that cradle yet? He didn't see it! He said we must visit Faneuil Hall. We asked him what nigger troupe was performing there now?

He looked bewildered. Then he said we must see where Warren fell. We asked him if Warren ever got over it—the place where he fell. He appeared demoralized. He said we must hear the big organ before we left Boston.

We went to hear the big organ. It is held in several buildings. It is one size larger than Boston.

Boston is the hub around which the organ revolves.

The organ is a revolver.

Like the organ, this is a big play on words.

People in New York and Buffalo hear the moan of the sea. The moan is the big organ.

It is used in mass!

It has a sort of *long* island sound!

Boston people go to Heaven through the big organ.

That is, when the nigger is out, so they cannot go through him.

There are but few gambling-houses in Boston. No such felloes are around that hub.

They don't play "straits" in Boston—not in the streets.

Harvard College is just beyond reach of the big organ.

Cambridge University is always in session. It is a law school. The pleading is done at the bar of the Parker House.

The studies at Cambridge are said to be very dry. They affect the pupils. Pleading at the bar affects them, likewise—or more like than wise.

No one ever gets lost in Boston. The city is so well *organ*-ized. Like the big organ, Boston has numerous stops! Some of the streets are nearly as long as a fish-pole; but not so long as a Johnson veto message. If a man don't like one street in Boston, it is easy to get on another one.

After four days' trial we could go from the

Parker House to the City Hall without getting lost! This is a fact. And in five days we learned the route from Scollay's Building to Engine House No. 4.

The business blocks in Boston are in shape like Norwegian shoes! The streets of Boston are like hop-poles struck by lightning. Some of them are so wide that a cow could be milked in them by turning her on her back, and sitting astride her brisket. Small horses are driven abreast—large horses tandem—in Boston. The fat woman was exhibited there once—in the big organ. Boston streets are not so crooked as they might be. The sun has warped them straight. Very clean in Boston. If a lady drops a pin from her clothes, policeman makes her pick it up. If a man shoots an apple seed out of a grocery, he is fined. Boston is very neat—especially near the big organ and cradle of liberty. If a man drops a remark, he is made to pick it up. And Boston people are *so* modest. They under-rate themselves terribly.

The streets of Boston must have been thrown in at the time of some big fire—they are so regular. If you would find any place, start in an opposite direction. If you see a policeman coming towards you, he is going the other way. If he runs from you he'll be where you are in no time. Up hill is down, and "over there" is "back here."

One day we started from the office of the Boston *Post* to the Boston post-office, seventy feet distant. We walked straight ahead—went around seven blocks—saw a policeman standing in a door-way on each block—asked each one the route to the post-office. Saw the eighth policeman, asked him politely. Said he, "Look here, this is the eighth time you've asked me that question! Move on, or up you go!"

Thought the policemen must be brothers—they looked so much alike! Rather than go around the block again we went t'other way, began to unwind, and got into the post-office by mistake. The front of a building is inside— in the courts.

Except the big organ and the cradle!

Ben. Butler spoke, while we were there, on the restoration policy.

Went to his meeting, expecting to see him giving back silver-ware and other valuables. Was mistaken. That kind of restoration wasn't policy!

House rents are cheap in Boston. Moving is cheaper than house rent. It's all owing to the hub, the big organ, and the cradle.

There is no drinking in Boston. No peculiar female characters. What is common is not peculiar.

New Bedford is to be moved into Boston soon. By legislative enactment, the mumps are to be confined to Democrats—the cholera is to trouble only foreigners—the chicken-pox is to be confined to old hens—niggers are to have straight hair to disgrace them—and the whites are to have curly wool on their craniums to make them popular in Boston. Not forgetting the big organ and the cradle of liberty!

New York is in the watch-fob, the South in the breeches pocket, and the West buttons on the tail of the coat of Boston.

The sun rises in Boston. The final conflagration of mundane things will begin in Boston, on account of the big organ and the cradle! Boston would have been laid out more regularly if the dogs of olden times had been pointers, or the cows had walked in more direct paths. Therefore we may see many calves in Boston. So much for tilting hoops!

A good place to move from—if one moves early.

From the cradle to the big organ,

Crookedly,

"Brick" Pomeroy.

CHAPTER IX.

How I lost Aurelia.

IE still, fond heart and sich, ye're thinkin' on her now! In a little box, this morning, old and blood-stained as 'twere by time, beside an old Testament, a slate pencil, and a little brass finger-ring, I found a tin top and wooden-bottom button, of the real old sort. Thirty years since I slung those buttons into them box, with a sigh of great size.

I was born at an early exclamation point of life, of poor but wealthy parents, and grew up to boy's estate on such food of love as mush and milk, pork and beans (subdued by caloric), chicken pot-pies, harvest apples, young milk—not intoxicable—and dreams. Dreams sustained me through the night, while the tall pines roaring without taught me to pine for some one—while the butter-nut tree across the road, dandling imaginary babies in the air, with its long limbs or arms, told me plain as tree could talk that I'd *butternot* live always without some one to dandle, and et cetery!

Yes! And so I loved, but knew it not! With my pants on the floor, my jacket thrown on the foot of the bed, my hat safely hove into a corner of my bedroom, how I dreamed the happy hours away till milking time. Ah, me! I was happy then, but not old enough to know it!

And I loved. Start not, gentle reader; but this is a fact. Aurelia Tillinghast was the rose I hummed around. She was three summers and somewhere near four winters older than I was at that time. But I caught up with her! She afterward married, and grew young soon after, and then I got the start of her. She had a father at the time I loved her, and before, too, for all I know. I said she was older. So she was. She was born of poor but wealthy parents; but the poor predominated to a severe muchness. She was part French—from Dublin. She was large. There was no other girl on the creek. Oh! I loved her as the deep blue tree loves the morning air; as the trout loves the briny deep; as the dog loves its midnight bark; as the infants

> On their mother's knee
> Drink and love their catnip tea,
> So I did love my Au-ril-ye!
> The only child of Tillinghas—t

And his wife! My folks said it was wrong; but love knew better. It wasn't much of a catch for either of us; but 'twas the best we could do! My folks didn't favor the alliance. Aurelia's derivatives, seeing in my little gait, in my sparkling eyes, light hair, and love for sass, much to admire, as it betokened genius, was willing.

So I used to run away, five miles through the woods, to see her who was so dear to me. And she used to fix up. I went six nights in the week. Every night Aurelia did wash her feet, and slip on her cowhide slippers. They looked red like, but 'twas all right, for pride is abominable. And being economical, Aurelia did not wear hose. Nature unadorned is adorned the most. And her hair! A very gentle mauve, without spot or blemish. Pure as the life of John Brown, straight as the mountain ash! Her face was—well it was all face—and her breath was like new-blown hay. Ah, how I loved her; who could help it! There was no more Aurelias within sixteen miles, for honest men with little girls in their families had not discovered the beauties of our woodland place of residence!

Aurelia's father liked the idea of wedlock

How I lost Aurelia.

concerning us. Aurelia had experienced twenty-two seasons of severe existence. Her father was a primitive artist, and played the march of civilization on the monarchs of the forest. He reaped the rich reward of twelve dollars a month and board for this pastime. My derivative was his employer. Hence the position! Aurelia had much appetite, and was expensive in this branch of education. Hence the desire. Drygoods were expensive, and Aurelia's father being like his daughter, a little fat, had great difficulty in making both ends meet. Hence the ambition of the Tillinghasts.

My father was more wealthier. He could brandish a watch on the Sabbath, slung from a genuine silk cord. And he had a satin vest, seventeen years old. And he had a pair of boots for Sabbath wear. And one griddle of the stove was always removed to furnish the wherewithal to polish those boots. I had to polish them. Hence my polish air and polished manner.

Every Sunday, at two o'clock, the stage came into the settlement seven miles up the creek. There were two horses to that stage, and at least once a month it had a passenger. Once it had two passengers—a man and dog. The man rode on the seat with the driver; the dog ran behind. That was a big day for Seely Creek. My father often spoke of it. He had been to the settlement every Sunday for four years. He was sick one day. 'Twas on that day the stage had two passengers. Father said it was just his luck. The people there talked about the stage for a long time. It waited an hour till father could arrive, but he didn't come. He was sick. He heard of it, and felt bad, but all the neighbors told him of it. And Tillinghast always went to the settlement with him. They used to talk about my marriage with Aurelia. Tillinghast went to the settlement that Sunday, as usual, and he, a poorer man than my father, saw the stage come in! My father did not see the stage come in, and the idea that Tillinghast did see it, created a coolness between them (even in July) they did not get over till January.

My father was a proud man—as he should have been, having such a son. So he told Tillinghast the match should be broken off. My father was a tall man, six feet four. Tillinghast was a little fat cuss, four feet six. They used to look up and down at each other. And that was the long and the short of it. The proposed wedlock was delayed. Tillinghast made offers. He offered to settle lots of property on his daughter. He, too, was proud, and eager for the fray—so to speak. I was tall, like my masculine derivative. Aurelia, like a dutiful girl, patterned after her papa. Filial affection is commendable, so I commendabled Aurelia. And everybody wants to marry in a high family.

But the stage affair damed the stream of neighborly affection existing between our paternals. Tillinghast was to blame—he said so. He offered to give Aurelia, on her wedding, a skillet without a handle; a half-dozen new sap troughs; a pair of red stockings, which should come to within an inch of her dress; a new splint broom; a wooden pancake turner, made out of water-beech, so that its natural limber would flap the cakes nicely; a top-knot hen; a wooden scoop-shovel, in which to take up dirt from the kitchen; a pair of his old pants to begin a rag carpet with, and a new fine-comb, left there by a pedler the year before in payment for supper, lodging, and breakfast for himself, horse, and wagon!

Father consented, and how happy I was! Hastened I to Aurelia and told her the news. We two turtle-doves sat on the edge of the spring, and paddled our feet in its limpid waters by moonlight, for hours. I never had kissed her before, for it is wrong to kiss girls—before you kiss them! But that night, how I went for kisses. We smacked and smacked, till the owls

"We two turtle doves sat on the edge of the spring and paddled our feet in its limpid waters by moonlight for hours. I had never kissed her before."—*Page* 78.

How I lost Aurelia. 79

hooted in fear. And I hugged Aurelia ever so muchly. We slipped into the spring, and hugged each other then; that was the first Aurelia ever knew of a waterfall; but it didn't make her proud.

* * * * At last a new stage-route was put on. It led by Aurelia's house. Her father's house did not have many mansions, but it was enlarged and made a stage house. And the stage stopped there over night. And that accomplished stage-driver was a mean cuss! I thought it then; I think it now. He was not handsome, like myself; but lordy, how he could crack a whip! Early in the morning he would get on a stump by the barn and snap that long whip till the hens and roosters would cackle for two hours! Aurelia's parents thought 'twas I kissin' Aurelia, but 'twan't!

And all this a heavy novelty was to that sweet little one. She had never experienced so much happiness previous. It was a new thing. Like some other people, new things proved to be her best game! And the whipper-snapper of a stage driver brought her candy all the way from Elmira, then called by the name of Newtown. And he did keep his hair greased! And essence of cinnamon brought he for those mauve-complexioned tresses, and essence of peppermint for her breath. He was an extravagant stagist! And it was by thus the serpent of that gay fellow's love stole into my temple, I thought him all-fired humbly. I often informed Aurelia to this end, but she could not discern it. He used to kiss her, and hug her, and I knew it. And she liked it! But what could I do? Aurelia was the first born! I bought a whip, and had a big snapper put on it, and nearly cut my ears off in the endeavor to crack it as fiercely as did Jehiel, for that was his name. But 'twas no use; the business was new, the snapper wouldn't snap, and Jehiel beat me!

The night we sat on the edge of the spring and hugged ourselves into it, I wanted to be liberal. I had nothing, so I gave Aurelia a button from my trowserloons. I had no knife to cut it off, so Aurelia chawed it off. And I took some of her hair, made a little string from it, and hung it around her neck. It was a charm with Aurelia's charms. She wore it near her heart. I was happy when she wore it, and often wished I was a little button with a tin top and wooden bottom, so I could hang around Aurelia's neck.

When the stage stopped at Tillinghast's he spruced up. He had my father then where the hair was short, and their affection took another cold. My father took a rheumatism in his limbs, and couldn't walk to the settlement, as he once could, to see the stage come in. So he went to walk down to the corner where Aurelia lived, to see it come in. Seeing stage come in was one of his best holts. And he used to ad mire Jehiel, who was the greatest whip-snapper in that county. He took pride in it. I grew to hate my father because he spoke well of Jehiel. Not of him, but of his whip-snapping. I felt bad and out in the hemlock pined to a shadow.

*　*　*　One day father come home. He handed me something tied up in a little piece of dirty cloth. I opened it. It was the button now before me. A simple button, but it did a tale unfold which rang in my ears worse than ever did Jehiel's whip! It bore the marks of Aurelia's teeth, where once, in maiden meditation, she had squoze a tooth in it, while chawing it off! It was a simple tin-top wooden-bottom button, but I hated it, and stamped it to the earth. Four little tears stood in the eyes of the button as it lay pressed in the moist earth. I took it up carefully, and laid it away, as I would Aurelia, and it has never been looked at till now. And I grew up to be

"Brick" Pomeroy.

P. S.—Aurelia got married, and her Jehiel is still stage-driving. "B." P.

CHAPTER X.

The Dog-Gondest Dog.

BURN the dorg! There goes a three-by-five feet pane of plate-glass out of a door, and there goes the cussedest and wussedest piece of excitable canine we *ever* saw! Four years ago, the day after a chap on the cars had the upper end of his *snoot* punched for calling us a traitor, Po. Hatcher gave us that red and brindle batch of dog, then done up small like, but looking so bull-dogish that we were afraid of his picture for a week! Po. said he was an Alabama bull-dog, imported from New Jersey in a basket, as a sample of the handsome of that country. But he was a pretty purp. His tail was no longer than a wicked man's prayer, and was full as stunin'! And those ears! They looked like a small corner of plug tobacco! And such eyes! And such eyebrows! When he was but a child, so-called, some monster must have slung him head-first against a stone wall! His jaws were pretty jaws. They were so severe in their angles. There was so much *jaw* in proportion to the purp, that we wanted to call him Swisshelm; but he wan't that kind of a pet! But he was nigh onto all jaw!

We kept him four weeks in the sanctum, and all that time hired a nigger to watch him. He'd steal—*steal* is no name for it! And he kept that nigger mighty busy watching him, till at last the nigger, being such a smart, mimicky, educationable cuss, got so much worse nor the dog, that we kept the dog to watch the nigger! Egad, wan't it a full team? Strange how niggers will learn things!

And he was the hungriest dog we *ever* saw! A pennyworth of beef didn't last him as long as a ten-dollar bill would a Democrat the night before election. He had a fine voice for beef. And what the dog would not eat, the nigger would! And the dog grew large, and ponderous about the jaws. He used to eat paper, books, mats, vests, old hats, gloves, patent-leather boots, window curtains, and sich. He ate such stuff for dessert. That dog ate a full calf-bound set of Harper's Weekly one day, just on account of the calf. And he ate ten copies of the Chicago *Tribune* one day, but the lie in them papers made him so dog-goned sick all that week that he would have died if the nigger in 'em hadn't emeticked 'em out, and so he got well! But he never pined himself to a shadow hankering after Republican newspapers any more. And he kept on stealing. We always thought them Republican newspapers aided the development of that complaint, for he was sure to steal all the nigger earned for us.

He'd walk out on a rainy day for his health, and always came back with something he'd *found.* Once it was a lady's veil. Then it was half a ham, with a butcher-knife sticking in it. What he wanted to bring the knife with him for is more than we know, unless he had to cut and run! One day he came in with a baby's cradle. There was some blood on the edge of it, and all that afternoon the bell-man was out ringing a bell and yelling, "Boy lost!" John Brown didn't go out for two or three days!

Once he came in with a wooden leg in his teeth. That night a wooden-legged soldier was missing; but as crippled soldiers were of no account, he didn't try to keep shy a bit. He brought us the leg, no doubt thinking it the kind of club we like for the La Crosse DEMOCRAT. And he used to steal money! He'd go into a store and snatch greenbacks out of a cash drawer, just as handy !

One day he came in with a contribution box he'd stolen from the entry-way of a close communion church. He carried the box behind the end of the sideboard, broke it open—*and looked sick !* John Brown never stole a contribution box again ; and after that, when we'd point to that box, and smile, he'd drop his tail—what there was of it—and look mean enough. And he'd steal halters, bridles, saddles, and such stuff. And as he grew older, he'd actually unhitch a horse and lead him across the line into Minnesota. When any one would call out, " John Brown," he'd go for a horse, sure. And so we had to change his name.

What to call the cuss we didn't know. But as he had chawed up so many books, and was always meddling with what was none of his business, and grew to be sort of dogmatic, and radical about his bloody jaws, we left off calling him John Brown, and called him Sumner. For a while he seemed to like it. He was a ambitious dorg, and to keep his name good, meddled with so much that was none of his business that at last he got a dog-goned caning, which so affected his backbone that we had to send for Anna Dickinson. After she strengthened up his spinal vertebræ, he howled and ranted around so we had to change his name again.

So well called him Curtiss. And that seemed to please him mightily. He'd stand on his hind legs before a glass, poke the hair out of his eyes, and when he went out doors he strutted about as though he was going to fight a Pea Ridge battle! And what notice he'd take of mules! He fell in love with mules! He became enamored of mules, and often would lead them to the outskirts of the city and hide them in the bushes. And he grew into such a taste for cotton. Never saw a dog so fond of cotton. In fact, he had such a love for cotton that 'twan't safe to let him walk on the street, nor stay in the sanctum, nor go to any place, so we called him Sigel. That bothered him. He had a tough time of it. Gracious, how he'd twist his jaws and bark! And he loved to get into a dog fight, too. He'd whip any dog in the city. But it took so long to get him in a fight, that he was useless. You see when we wanted him to fight one dog, we'd set him to fight another one, and then he'd back into the t'other one, then fight his way out! But it took so long to learn his style; and then 'twan't always convenient to get up two fights, so we changed his name again.

He grew beautiful each day. In fact, he was a handsome cuss! And folks took so much notice of him he forgot he was nothing but a poor dog, and he acted so that we thought best to call him Butler.

You never saw such a change come over a dog. He grew cunninger and cunninger every day. He'd go to butcher shops, rub his paws on the carcass of a dead beef, and come home to make us believe he'd been fighting. And as he growled so when he came, and never had any cuts or wounds on him, we thought he was getting to be terribly brave. But at last we found him out. And how that dog would strut! And he grew mean. He'd drive small dogs away from their bones, and got to chasing kittens to some point out of harm's way. And he'd snap and snarl at women—always insulting them. And he had half-a-dozen pups he'd picked up around the city, as mean but not as smart as he; and these pups would chase poor girls into some corner where he would scowl, bark at, and then, after rubbing his dirty nose over them, leave them with some wound on them. But when he heard a gun, Lord bless you, how he'd run, and hold his tail close between his legs! We had lots of trouble with him. When he saw a church, he wanted to go in and steal something. And when he saw a telegraph report in the office, he looked as if he wanted to change it some way. The only thing he was fit for was to watch jewelry stores! Let that dog go by a show-window where there would be some silver-ware, and he'd stand around there all day. And he'd look into store windows, and break into churches to look at the communion plate. And he'd follow a funeral for miles, if there was a silver plate on the coffin. Most folks thought he was always one of the mourners. But when we found that the graves were dug into, and one day saw his kennel filled with silver plates, screws, etc., gnawed from coffin-lids, we knew what a vehement mourner Butler was. A funeral procession just passed the door—and that is what the dog-goned dog went out for so quick!

If anybody wants a red and brindle, square-jawed pet of this kind, whose keeping will not amount to over five or six hundred dollars a month, unless we have to pay for his stealings, we'd like to sell him. He is a sweet pet—just such a purp as some poor man who is not able to buy a window-curtain or a book for his wife to read, would want. He can eat a horse and chase the rider up a tree any day, and were it not for his peculiarities, would be a fine dog. He'll eat anything, from an inkstand to a linen night-shirt—from a pound of candles to a baby—from a magazine to an india-rubber boat, and grows more handsome every day he lives. We'll sell him cheap. For particulars address, with revenue stamp to prepay return postage on the dog, which is such a handy thing to have about yours most dog-goned truly,

"Brick" Pomeroy.

CHAPTER XI.

Peter Oleum struck by "Brick."

PETROLEUM! You are the Pete for me! Else why! Mr. Moses smote the rock, and water gushed forth, first; I smote its rock, and exceeding much of oil trickled forth. And I am rich oilso. To find such much of a greace, doth well a-grease with me. I skirmished from garret upon oil region. Ever since I became born, my poverty has been hard to be borne! I have suffered—I have been bored by creditors! My credit was run into the ground. People thought me rich, meanwhile, and a very meanwhile it was, too! They

thought I had plenty of money; so they wanted pay down for what I bought. Not wishing to humor people, albeit something of a humorous, perhaps I would not purchase many things. I leased, I bored, I brought it! Veni, vidi, vici! Oili-ile-si-greased. Oils well that ends well; especially if it is an oil well! I bored, and it came. I drilled a hole through a rock; and oilready have been rewarded with so much of the fuel being prepared for the final conflagration, that I fear the last boil will end in as great a fizzle as did the Dutch Gap Canal.

And now I am rich—more rich than any man, or any other man. I have lots of money now, when I have no use for it. What a queer world! Nothing like oil! Folks say, "Hallo, here's Hon. Mr. Brick just struck a fortune. Deuced fine fellow, Mr. Brick!" Three months since I was plain "Brick." It oil owing to Petroleum.

And now for a splurge. Brown stone house

on Fifth avenue, with brown stone front, designed by old Brown himself, on both ends of it. Red horses with green tails, pink eyebrows, blue ears, chocolate-colored eyes, frizzled mane, and matchless style. Yellow wagon with black sides, purple blinds, and brown top, à la clam shell. Ethiopian driver with white kids, solferino stockings, magenta hat band, and false teeth on gutta-purcha base. And a sixty-four ox-stave ethiopiano, with brocatelle drawers, that modesty may not be shocked by looking at the legs thereof. And a library devoted to red-backs, yellow-backs, brown-backs, maroon-backs, and even "greenbacks!" Darn the expense, quothes I! And I'll have a park in the woodshed, and a bathing-tub full of the oil in church, and a wild buffalo to cut steak from, and oysters as large as Lincoln's majority, and boots with round toes and square heels, and a seat in some fashionable church, and new hoop-skirts for all my hired girls, and I will employ so many niggers to wait on me, that oil I'le have to do will be to be happy. Oh, Pete! let me kiss you for your Ma! And I'll lay a-bed mornings, and I'll sit up oil night, and bore my friends oil day, till they can't bare-l it! Talk about honest industry, sawing wood for the dust, opening oysters for the shells, blacking boots merely to see your face in them, and being honest forty years waiting for some rich man to adopt you! Played! Petroleum is the boy. And now I'll live high. Out of the house, vain pomp! Away from me, cold cuts, crackers, cheese, mush boiled, No. 5 mackerel, warmed-up soup, and brilliant appetites! I've struck Pete!

Now, when I go on the street, folks run to the window and smile. And they smile at me on the street. And they ask me to smile in Ginuel Cock Tail's house. And they all have a kind word! O, Pete! You're the Roleum for me! Things in my limited kingdom isn't as they use to once was! Farewell, ragged habiliments!

Good-by, hungry stomach! Oil River, cold shoulders! It's oil right, now. Ten years ago, Buggins wouldn't speak to me, 'cause I was not well, financially speaking. Buggins is now as cordial as horse-radish or hot whiskey. And when I would wedlock those rich girl, who so sweetly was unto me, her cruel parients said, "Oh, poor but honest youth, entice thyself hence!" And I enticed—nobody! Now, those girl, and those cruel parients wish me to call. How are you, bettered circumstances? It is good to remember oil these things! And the time dwells in those fond recollections of mine, as how I was not wanted at fashionable parties. Now the doors fly wide, and ebony angels of shoddy swing the panels for me to enter and revel. O Pete! you're oil right, my boy!

Money! More than would wad a columbiad! Everybody is willing to trust me, now. I have no need for credit. Rich folks are deuced glad to see me. They bow very low to me, now.

They didn't once. Great is Peter Oleum, and boring is its profit! Just to think of it. How I used to once dig potatoes on shares—turn grindstones for fun—milked cows for the buttermilk—cotton strings for suspenders—boss's old boots or freeze toes—hired man's hat or get tanned—second table or not at all—"dirty-fingered typesticker," or poor mechanic—go afoot or stay behind! Oil is a dream now. Stare, hilarious days, for poverty are over, and shoddy is, indeed, envious!

Guess I can kiss Matilda Jerusha, now, and her dad won't object, for I've struck ile! Reckon tailor will have time to make those raiments for I this week. Think landlord won't insist upon moving out of his abode. Things is working now. Another vein is opened! And you don't know how nice it is. If I go on a "bum," folks look over it, now. When I was poor, they looked into it. I can kick bootblacks, snub poor people, break car windows, throw goblets at waiters, hurrah for any man I like, wink at whose wife I wish to, tie my team to shade trees, stand on church cushions with dirty feet, jam people's hats down over their eyes, tell a man he is a liar, spit on the carpet, get drunk or sober, swear or not, as I please, and its oil right, for I've struck Pete! And I can sit up oil night, and raise much h—armony. No one objects. Mrs. Stiggings says I is the nicerest man she ever sawed. Mrs. Piggerly says I is the most delightingest gentlemen she ever knowed. The Stiggins and Piggerly girls say I am mostly exquisitious! It's oil on account of Peter Oleum, who has lately come to see me.

And I'm "on it," now. Have left my measure for a set of diamonds the size of a coal bed. And I have ordered silk shirts, satin stockings, more antique elastics, and a gold shaving-cup. And I'll have a guitar, harp, organ, piano, and tinkling cymbal in the house, oiled with petroleum, so they will play easy. And my hair, my whiskers, my pocket-handkerchiefs, my big clothes and my little clothes, shall bask in a barrel of petroleum while I sleep. O Pete, I'm fixed at last! I'll found a church, or founder a horse. I'll buy a horse-railroad, and run it with petroleum; hire religious editors to puff me into Christianity; buy a nomination for a fat office, and become as stiff as oil-boiled silk. Go away, poverty, I am wearied of your caresses! You have a large society, but I don't appreciate your grip. Your by-laws are right, but against my constitution. Now I can give advice, and it will be heeded. It's nice to have struck ile—one has so many more friends than he ever thought for, and people take such an interest in you. I can go on 'Change, buy a few thousand shares on call, sell gold, long or short, deal in stocks at buyer's option, have a private box at the opera, shake hands with old Mr. Nabob, and sing what tune I please. Young man, bore for oil! Strike Pete, and be happy! Cause the earth to gush into your lap, and beauty will gush oil over thee. Strike oil and be great!

The question once was, who inflicted a blow under the auricular of William Patterson. Farewell, Pat! The interrogation now is: "Who struke Pete?" I've struck him, and once more am happy. If society wants to come forward and take a new brother's hand, society can now do it. If young ladies of fashion wish to carry me sweetly once ere I become die, they will please step forward, and not rumple my clothes! If any seeker after notoriety wishes to kiss me for the Sanitary, they can now do it, and one of my niggers shall hold the stakes. I've struck Pete, and the result is much gorgeousness of apparel—many good things heretofore known to me only by observation.

I would not be a poor man—
I would not if I could—

But I need not fret about it,
For I could not if I would,

while the earth divulges its hidden secrets into my lap at the rate of three hundred barrels. Its oil right, now. Once I was merely a bore. Now I am a successful borer, and my troubles have been drowned in oil by the genius of success—Peter Oleum. Oilways thine,

"BRICK" POMEROY.

CHAPTER XII.

TEUTONIC ANGUISH.

A FEW years since the country remembers that a steamer, the *Lady Elgin*, was lost on the trip from Chicago to Milwaukee, and about three hundred persons on board were drowned. The first report was that all had perished; but several escaped and returned to their homes, after an absence of from one to three days. There lived at Milwaukee, at that time, a burly German, named Triheister Dotswinger, who rejoiced in a three-cornered lager-beer saloon, an eight-square vrouw, and an oval-faced cherub of eighteen summers, boy

by nature, Schneider Dotswinger by name, and graceful as a young bologna-sausage in all its pristine bloom.

Schneider coaxed his two derivatives to go on the ill-fated steamer. News came that she was lost. The anguish-stricken Teuton, in a paroxysm of grief, called on us in the editorial rooms, to inquire about his boy. We told him—as we were informed—that all were lost, and of course his boy was a goner. He seated himself on a pile of books, and thus held forth:

"Mein Gott! mein Gott! Mr. Bumroy! 'tis always shust so as it never vash since it vash so, und I knows em! I have so mooch droobles dis day as never vash since I make start mit mine lager peer grocery. It is shust so all der time, and I feels so pad *all down here* mit mine pelly! Lut us go und make some laerg peer drink, und I dells you pout dat Schneider vot shust now lost me in ter Lady Helshin!"

We accompanied the grief-stricken one to a

saloon where lager was held forth, and over a glass of the beverage he thus continued:

"Now, Mr. Bumroy, mine heart be aus ka spielt (played out). I make so mooch loves ver dat Schneider as vot no man never makes for his poy. I'se had so mooch droobles mit him, doo. Ven he vas un fine leedle poy, fat, shust like un leedle pig, he had so mooch worms ash no poy never had, and it dakes more as zwei barrels of goot lager peer to get dat poy out of der worms. *Take some more peer, Mr. Bumroy!*

"Und den, mine friend, he makes take der leedle meesels, and goomes out all over in un solid leedle sphots, shust like un papy vot is so freckled as never vash; und it cost me more as doo tollars to get dat Schneider away from dem shpeckles. Und I makes play mit him on der vloor und have such fun shpankin him as never vash, und den he makes mooch grow und goes out ter door ven he vants too, shust like no pody, so it does his poor fadder's heart so mooch goot tc vatch him ash you never saw! *Take some more peer, Mr. Bumroy!*

"Und den he make grow shust like notinks. Und he gets so pig in his leedle sthumach like his fadder! He vas shust such a poy ash never vash. Und he makes himself grow pig, und he drinks so much lager peer as his fadder, und is so much help in mine grocery. He draws peer so goot as I does, und I sits all ter dime seeing Schneider draw peer, und I smokes mine bipe to shleep all ter viles! Und now I feels so pad down here! *Take some more peer, Mynheer Bumroy!*

"Und now dat Schneider vas gone make himself drown on der Lady Helshin! He vosh so goot poy as never vash, and I must make myself get unodder little Schneider shust like him. I dell you, Mynheer Bumroy, I never make myself veel so pad since dat boy vas notink!"

Just then the door opened, and in came Schneider, a living witness fresh from the disaster, brought up by Dennison on the cars.

"Oh, mein Gott! he.e goomes dat Schneider!" Jumping up. "Oh, Schneider, you tamm rascal! Kiss your fadder! Goom to your poor fadder's arms!" They embrace. "Now take some lager peer mit your fadder. Go kiss your mudder, you tamm rascal! Here, kiss your fadder, you tamm rascal, vot drowns der Lady Helshin! Und you tamm rascal, ven next you goes mit der Lady Helshin to ride, you sthay here und sell lager peer, and lets your poor fadder go have funs not by a tamm sight! Oh, mein Gott! how I makes love dat poy! *I'd radder find fifty tollars in gold* as drown him mit ter steamboat!"

CHAPTER XIII.

"Brick" and the Deacon's Hexa.

DEACON BRIGHTWATER lived in New Hartford, Nutmeg State. He had a red house, a red horse, a red barn, red fence, a red cow, red window sash, an old-fashioned red sleigh, a red smoke-house, red hogs, little red eyes, and a red nose—the very picture of a New England Puritan. He had a wife who wore a red petticoat, and had the readiest tongue a woman ever fired at us. He had some little ready money, got by making cider brandy from stolen apples, and taking toll from the copper-spattered contribution saucer he passed in the red church in that settlement of Sunday beans, week-day onions, and orthodox views.

And he had a female child, whose name was Hexa Brightwater, and who was twenty-nine years old; wore red stockings, red garters, metal-tipped shoes, green spectacles, and the prettiest red hair the world ever set eyes on or into. Hexa, a true New England gal, chewed wads of pine gum, and sweetened her breath with onions. Hexa wasn't so much handsomer than a doll as to make the doll faint; but she was intelligent. In fact, intelligence was her best hold, but one; she was great on making baby garments, and had two trunks full packed away, that she might be ready as willing when the evil hour drew nigh, as she trusted it would, from year to year.

My father was a common sort of a rooster, and lived outside of the drippings of New England blessings. He was taught that in no other place could there be found women of intelligence, and he sent me there to find a loving lass, to court some intelligent beauty, to woo some refined nutmeggress, and with her return to my rural home to astonish the barbarians with something beyond the average of female loveliness.

I went to the Land of Steady Habits. I wanted to hand several "Bricks" down to posterity, and was told by father that with a New England girl for a wife I could raise more children, grow more onions, skin more eels, sing more psalms, know more of what was going on in the neighborhood, hear more scandal, sleep less nights, have more relatives, eat more beans, love myself and hate others more, and get more out of a dollar, than with any other sort of a woman in this happy country, so-called.

Deacon Brightwater, with his bright red nose, was a cunning man. He was a New England Christian. He crowded nineteen eggs under a fourteen-egg hen, always borrowing the five odd eggs! He smelt of peoples' breath to see if they had been drinking liquor, and then made a few stamps, as a Connecticut Good Templar spy, by informing against them. He didn't drink himself, but got his nose tinted by holding it so close to the mouths of those who did! He split matches to make them last longer. He'd pick up hen's heads to boil them for the fat thereon. He'd take a claw-hammer, when he went visiting, to draw tacks from carpets when unseen. He made cider-brandy, and made it on shares. He was always trying to swap horses, but never could find one that worked well on his machine; so he tried each one until noon, and sent them home hungry! He was a careful, prudent, whole-souled, liberal, spontaneous edition of benevolence, who gave his hogs' tails and rams' horns to the poor, and made prayers longer than the sweep of his cider mill, but, like that instrument, always pointed down.

Hexa Brightwater never had a beau till I visited her. She was too intelligent for the common herd. She knew everything. She could tell how long a wad of gum would last, how much a Southerner made from a nigger, how many duck eggs would hatch under a two-year-old pullet, and when beans were fit to bake. She was one of those higher sphere beings, who could do no wrong; who could not endure those who did.

How I did spark Hexa! Deacon Brightwater heard that I had wealth, and he was willing. He'd go to bed early. He'd play snore so Hexa and I would hurry up. Mrs. Deacon Brightwater went to sleep, too. She crawled in beside the deacon—front side. Their bedroom door was always shut by particular request of Hexa. She knew why it should be closed. I used to hear a footfall on the bedroom floor. I mistrusted Hexa's mother used to watch at the key-hole. She could see where Hexa and I sat to squeeze each other's hands, eat candy, and taste of each other's lips. I didn't like to have her do this. So one night, when I mistrusted, I slipped up beside the door and jabbed a wire into the key-hole. It was a long wire. I heard somebody squeal inside. She died before morning from the effects of that playful, Puritanical jab! That wire cured the key-hole disease. It opened the old lady's eye! The deacon followed her to the grave. With true New England affection he put up a tombstone, on which was—

> Hic jacket Hexa's Mother,
> Orphan child without a brother.
> She went hence with a single eye, &c.,
> And left I single to go forth!
> Tears cannot restore her,
> Therefore I weep!
> As I pile sod o'er her
> All in a heap.

The deacon grow pale, all except his nose. That wouldn't pale. It was in better spirits. The deacon married a nigger lady from the cotton country, and was happier than ever. Then Hexa and I had it all our way. We'd sit in the parlor, I cross-legged, Hexa with one foot under her, like a duck. She was strong minded. She wanted heaps of hugging, and you bet I was old industry at that business. She used to begin our Sunday night devotion by singing—

"Arm me with jealous care!"

I used to arm her, every time! She liked it. Then she would read a chapter about how the waste places should be made glad. I used to make her waist places glad, lots, till my arms got so tired I couldn't. Then she'd pillow her head on my manly chest, and I'd pillow my head on her manly chest. And we agreed that all I had should be hern, and all she had should be mine. She thought mine was more than hern, but it wan't. Her dad was rich.

I used to help her weed onions. That was her

strong game. She'd snatch an onion bed bald-headed in four minutes. She never missed a weed. She knew clover from onions just as easy. When they all grew in one clump, she'd dissect them quicker than a cat could lick her ear. I've seen her snatch for a handful of weeds right in among the onions, and never faze an un! The old deacon said once, as I stood in the barn holding a sheep for him to shear, that there was a consolation in affliction, for he had buried six wives and felt that each one was a stepping-stone over the river to glory. He paused his shearing, looked skyward up alongside a black bottle he carried in a side pocket, and resumed his clipping. I saw by his nose that he was affected. I pitied him. I asked him if the river was broad. He said it was, and deep. I asked him if his stepping-stones reached, as yet, near the glory shore. He said not quite—about half way. I looked at the humpy old deacon and his bald head, and as I got sight of his new wife, asleep in the sun on the wood-pile, surrounded by a swarm of admiring flies, anxious to kiss her for her mother, but too polite to touch her opened lips, I reverently thought, "Old Cocky, it will be a wonder if the nigger don't beat you and plant you first as the next step-stone."

We sheared the sheep. Then we sat under the fence, and while I tied my shoe I could hear a gurgle about the deacon's mouth. I thought it was his nose preparing to blossom, but it was only cider-brandy.

And we sat there and talked until the noon-hour came. We settled our marriage matters, and I was to have Hexa, if I could get her. There was a question about the dowry. The deacon wanted me to pay the funeral expenses of his last wife; not but he was glad to get rid of her, but he found her more expensive after death than before. I refused to pay for such nonsense. He found that I was in earnest, and let up. If he hadn't, after all I'd spent for

Hexa, in the way of time and travel, I'd have gone for his red knob, and he knew it.

By and by the old deacon fell asleep, and I went in to comfort Hexa. We had a nice time. She was a rapid talker. I was a mere man of mud in comparison to her. She knew she was smart. She knew all other women were ignorant, for she had been taught it. I didn't love her for her love, but for her hate. She hated everything beyond her eyeshot. She hated some parts of New England, not because onions wouldn't grow there, but because in some places there were great, ugly Democrats, and they kept increasing. But I didn't want a woman to love me—only one who was intelligent—and so I sparked her.

Our marriage-day was fixed. Being an ignorant Western laborer, I was forced to agree to remain a servant in that household ten years, to get the hang of their notions.

I had to learn to use a sickle instead of a reaping machine—to use psalms instead of melodies—to woik for others instead of myself. It was all right, for a while. But I couldn't love the deacon's dusky wife. Did not like her color. And when I wanted to hunt, I had to shoot straight up into the air, or down into the well, for fear of trespassing. And when I wanted to run and expand my lungs, I was plum against a stone fence in less than a minute. If I kissed Hexa on the Sabbath, I was fined for it. I was forced to drink cider-brandy, or nothing; and I was fed on onions till I sickened of them. Onions are good for two or three hundred meals, but for a steady diet, I like them not. I tried to love Hexa; but as soon as she found I was betrothed to her, she put on airs. She made me hew her wood, draw her water, find her in food, and pay extra for sewing on my shirt buttons, making neckties, and all such little jobs.

And I had to work hard all day carting apples from other farms for Deacon Brightwater to grind up into apple cider to redden his nose. And if I wanted a drink of cider I had to pay for it from over-work. And I had to work to fix up the little garden patch—to repair his old mill that wasn't worth repairs. As the old deacon grows old he grows mean. As Hexa thinks she has got a fellow tight, she just everlastingly goes for him. I am the best worker ever on the place. I make the old farm, so-called, valuable, and it is for Hexa's interest to keep me. But she hates me—she is jealous of me—she don't try to make it pleasant for me—she quarrels with me, and says I am nothing but a great ugly brute. She scolds me till I could almost die, steals my trinkets, cuts up my clothes for rag carpets; and whenever she goes to a tea-party, she tells folks what a mean cuss I am and what a sweet intelligent angel she is.

Some day I'll quit on Hexa—we'll go through that old cider-brandy mill, and leave for the

West, where I can see daylight without being obliged to look straight up, and where I can find some one better natured, if not so smart to sew on buttons and make neckties. I'll work on—but keep getting my little duds in shape—and some day be off in earnest, and let the deacon sing his psalms, and let Hexa weed her onions. Thoughtfully thine,

"BRICK" POMEROY.

CHAPTER XIV.

Cure for a Cold.

I HAVE been very sick. It was a cold. A dab bad cod id de ed. I came near going for to quit. I went so far down the lane, it was a grave question whether it were best to retrace or trace ahead. I caught it ever so easy. The fire went out. The lamp flickered low. The kitchen clock tolled the death of the day as I told the girl I loved her. The clock struck as the idea struck me I was getting cold. I told the girl so. We sat on a sofa. Said she, "Sit up closer." In her lap we laid our head. Who cared for a little cold? We talked of lots.

Cure for a Cold. 123

We talked low, because we were down-stairs. I caught the cold, but not the girl. Then I went to a doctor—a doctor of physic—so I met-a-physic! How do you like that joke? He felt of my tongue and looked at my pulse; said I was sick. Told me to go home, soak my feet, cover up in bed, eat nothing for a week, and be well. Gave him five dollars and saw my landlord. He said no deductions could be made on board, so I couldn't follow my physic's advice. Then I saw another doctor. He told me to take two bottles of hot drops, a bed-blanket covered with mustard, and go to bed. Told him I didn't want a hot drop till I dropped in forever. Told him I didn't want to be mustered in that way. Told him I didn't want to go to bed. Then I saw another knight of the scalpel. It was the same night that I saw him, though. He told me to take cod-liver oil and honey. Told him I had no cod liver. Then he said I must eat cold tallow. Said I, "That never agrees with me." Then he told me to eat fat beef. I thought him a humbug, and went elsewhere. Thought I'd try the cold-water plan. Eminent hydrantopothist told me to soak my head in ice-water; soak my feet in ice-water; sit in a barrel of ice-water two hours; bathe my back in ice-water; eat pounded ice till I sweat, and I'd feel better. Good way to get up a sweat; but then it would have spoiled a skating-pond to have done it.

Another doctor told me to use dumb-bells. Supposing he meant a deaf and dumb girl, I declined. Another Esculapius told me the homœopathist style was all the rage. Gave me five thousand little pills, marked A. Gave me five thousand more little pills, marked B. Gave me five thousand more little pills, marked C. Told me to take one pill in a pail of water every five minutes; to take another pill in two pails of water every four minutes. Told me to take half of another pill in five pails of water every two minutes. Took two pills and went to the

Cure for a Cold.

river. Hired a boy to dip up and pour down. Emptied the river in ten minutes. Changed my base to a young lake, and went at it again. Cold didn't improve—that is, the cold didn't improve me. Went home mad. Gave fourteen thousand pills to a chap who pilfered chickens from the barn. He still lives.

Another doctor told me to take calomel. Another told me to drink hot whiskey. How do you like that? Two good doctors. Glad I met-a-physics in such spirits. Sent two barrels of whiskey to my room. First tried a pint of hot whiskey. It loosened my eyes. Then I tried a pint of cold whiskey. It fixed them all right. Then I moved with great vigilance upon a pint of hot whiskey. It loosened my legs. Then I threw my left flank around a pint of cold whiskey. Felt better. Then I tried some hot whiskey. Fine doctors. Rather like them both. Tried some more cold whiskey. It affected my head, somewhatly. Tried another pint of hot whiskey. Very fine doctors—know just how to cure a cold. Shall employ them by the year. Tried two pints of cold whiskey. Began to feel better; felt like another man. Fine doctors; I love them quitely. Kept on with the whiskey; felt like three or four new men; but there never lived such good doctors. Tried half a quart of cold whiskey mixed with half a quart of hot ditto. Ditto always means whiskey. Felt better; felt like a company of new men. Tried to get in line; formed in shape of a hollow square on the floor. Took some more whiskey; don't remember whether it was hot or cold, or cold or hot. Felt much better. Passed a vote of thanks to the physicians; felt better. Drank to their health; got the whiskey mixed. Felt like a brigade of new men. Tried to surround my enemy. Moved upon his works, and he gave me bottle. Took another position. Threw my entire corps to the front. Attacked the commissary camp, and took a pint of whiskey pris-

"Drank to their health; got the whiskey mixed. Tried to surround my enemy. Moved upon his works and he gave me bottle."—*Page 126.*

oner. Fine doctors; like their way of curing colds. A good way; was five days proving it to be a good way. Hair pulls a little, but it was on account of the cold. They said I'd feel like a new man, and I believe them. When you have a cold, try the new style.

Spiritually,
"BRICK" POMEROY.

CHAPTER XV.

"Brick" Pomeroy sends the President his Ann-Alice.

NOTHING like being known as a scientific personage. Abraham read that I had struck "Peter," and forthwith, on returning from the Peace Conference, thus arrested my attention:

White House, Feb. 12, '65.

"*Successful 'Brick:'*—Your striking 'Pete' reminds me of a little story, and you are hereby authorized to march upon some oil section, examine the country, find oil, analyze it, and report forthwith to me. You will travel incog., at owner's risk, at your own expense, and I will

Sends the President his Ann-Alice. 129

settle the bill. See in your explorations that nobody is hurted. A. LINCOLN."

Protected, authorized, and commanded by this document, set out, armed with witch hazel-rods, a large gimlet, a string of auger holes to drive down, pair of opera glasses, the amnesty oath with sugar in it, pair of brogans reaching to the knees, four reams of foolscap, a trunk full of greenbacks, cigar box full of clothes, and much rectitude in those heart of mine concerning the Petrolia Bory Alis, for which I was to make light for this wicked world. Arrived on the spot which General Dix once proposed to shoot a man on, I pitched my tent, took the oath diluted with hot water and sugar, became intent on the bore, and proceeded with my procedure. First went through the rod, nature's greenbacks when the moon is right.

At fifty feet, struck a strata of Egyptian marble, in which dead Ethiopian frogs, mer-

6*

maids, and such works of art were imbedded and petrified with astonishment.' At seventy feet, passed through a deserted Indian village. At ninety feet, struck a balloon which had Chinese hieroglyphics on the bottom, bound up. At ninety-six feet, bored through a country school-house, where a girl of nineteen sat in a petrified state, oiling her hair with petroleum. At one hundred and ten feet, passed two dogs imbedded in solid rock, guarding a baby, which evidently had been rocked to sleep, as it was exceedingly much dead! Twenty feet further down, an obstacle so hard presented itself that I could not drive the auger hole, so was obliged to resort to a yard of drilling. Brought up a little wool, some thick pieces of skull, from which I was led to the belief that I had struck the head of a sable son of Ham. If so, I beg the pardon of the defunct Hammer.

At the depth of two hundred feet I struck a cooper shop, and from this judged oil was not far below, so advanced with caution. Ten feet further down I ran into a gin-mill, and felt in better spirits. At the depth of two hundred and fifty feet, struck a bottle of old rye. I knew civilization was not far distant, and waited. Soon a reliable contraband came along, and said I was oil right, and by urging my auger holes thirty feet farther into the stomach of the earth, I should be rewarded. I never can forget the debt of gratitude to this poor, down-trodden brother, who so kindly was unto me, and who I love so very much! Reliable contraband! I caressed him sweetly for the feminine half of his immediate ancestry, and drove on with my bore! I passed several valuable sections of farming land, rivalling the prairies of Illinois; a few stratas of property resembling Connecticut stone fence; some loyal streaks, which proved to be coal; several gold and silver lodes; sandstone and slate enough to furnish all of Brigham Young's children; salt water, in tiers, and a variety of photographic views of eminent roosters belonging to this or to some other world.

At the depth of two hundred and eighty feet, I struck a rich vein of patriotism. I looked for the model military man, Butler, as I went down; but met some victims coming up, who said he was down so low that no mortal could reach him, no matter how fast he drove his bore. Six feet further down I struck a box of Continental currency, on which green mildew was rapidly gathering; and several settlements of freed negroes, relieved from bondages since the war began.

At the depth of three hundred and seven feet nine inches and a fraction over a fifteenth, I struck Pete very much in the crude state, and now glory in a well which spurts seven hundred barrels of crude, and nine hundred barrels of refined petroleum, every six minutes. And the well is not yet in active operation. On analyzing the precious liquid, I find it to contain, in the crude state, two thousand parts, as followeth, to wit:

Peter	2	Nigger boarding-house	65
Oleum	4	Opera	18
Oil	3	Country residence	22
Diamond dust	20	Good opinion of neigh-	
Store clothes	19	bors	300
High living	86	Greenbacks	700
Patriotism	1	Watering-places	100
Fast horses	70	Internal revenue	2
Brown stone house	64	Neglect of poor relatives	19
Champagne suppers	90	Hilarious nights	26
Headache next morning	95	Poodle dogs and ser-	
Crinoline	21	vants	30
Cushioned pews	14	Genuine comfort	800
Style	11		

Total Ann-Alices 2,000

I have tried the crude Peter in my family with most gratifying results. It is good for all the ills flesh has an heir to, and a margin over for to-morrow. It will cure croup, plumbago, chronic inebriation, Dutch Gap Canals, corns, onions, leaks in boots, sore head (for politicians), fevers of all kinds, cancer on the pocket, bald-headedness, tight boots, and is the great instantaneous cure for all poverty, even in the most hopeless stages, or on foot, for that matter. Applied according to directions, it will sweep carpets, write letters, play faro, drive fancy horses, read late novels, visit opera, cause hair to grow on a boot heel, cut finger-nails, answer the door-bell, unlock hearts, brush clothes, mend watches, make champagne cocktails, edit newspapers, collect old bills, embroider cloaks, pick out the best cuts in market, sweep the streets, pick teeth on steps of fashionable hotels, make stump speeches, deliver lectures, kiss all the girls, cut out ladies' slippers, catch a pickerel, run a steamboat on the Upper Mississippi in time of drouth, write obituaries for Bethel fishermen, elect second-rate men to office, shut up your neighbors' eyes and mouths, and all on one application.

The refined article is still more wonderful

Applied gently, it will paint a lady's cheek. plumpify her fair form and figure, play the piano, ornament the walls, cure drunkenness, secure prayers from the clergy, make old clothes as good as new, cure fits, gout, blues, repinings; put marble floors in dwelling-houses, match horses, color gray hair and whiskers jet black, varnish faults invisible, and keep pocket full of cash. There is no perfume like it in the world, especially in the crude state!

I find also that for the cure of broken hearts it has no equal. Two doses will cure a boy of using tobacco. Applied with a feather, it will saw wood, hoe corn, pour molasses on hot pancakes, dodge behind the door after kissing another man's wife, husk oysters, divorce clam shells, crack butternuts in farmer-boy style, hatch chickens from wooden eggs, shut hot stove doors, cure jealousy, mend burnt dresses, frizzle hair, teach a minister to make short prayers when there are no cushions on the pew seats, give fashionable children lessons in politeness, pay salaries of country preachers more promptly, and protect army chaplains from camp evils. It will also solve chess problems, point horse nails as well as jokes, make cider, and play the violin.

From developments being made, I expect to be able in a week to report that: add to the comfort of boarding-houses, carpet church aisles, soften sleeping-car berths, keep tobacco-chewers from soiling carpets, restore peace, lessen the price of gold, bolster up damaged reputations, marry old maids, find homes for war widows, make conductors honest, keep women from gossip, curl straight hair, and give free passes on all railroads. Such is my Ann-Alice of Peter Oleum. With assurances of my most formidable distinguished consideration, and the highest personal regard for Your Highness, and

Sends the President his Ann-Alice.

hoping these few lines, which I take my pen in hand to hope you will enjoy the same blessing I have the pleasure to submit my Ann-Alice for Oil for Science.

"Brick" Pomeroy

CHAPTER XVI.

"Brick" and Kalista.

THOSE other girl of ours, as we are informed by letter, has done gone and got well locked unto a tinkerist of the gospel who attends prayer-meetings, swaps horses, stands chaplain in the army, and gets drunk on the sly! Oh, dear! This is much misery! Wherefore shall we flea go unto now? How we used to do courting for those girl. Candy, peanuts, lozenges, peppermint drops, little balls of honey-soap, night blooming for seriousness, and such evidences, did we pour into them lap of hers whereon at vesper chimes this head of ours did erst so sweeterly rest. Oh, dear! 'Twas all O K—ista!

We used to blacken our boots, starch our hair, grease our shirt, and curl our eyebrows for them girl. And we rode horse for her paternal derivative to cultivate corn; and we milked the brindle heifer as what no other boy could milk; and we split oven-wood—and who would not?—for her ma.

And at night, when bats came forth, and tumble-bugs crawled over the lea, and young pullets sat in maiden meditation fancy free, holding their head under one wing so as to learn love by hearing their hearts beat, we would hasten under Kalista's window, and she would, with her lily-white hand, snail us up by the hair till we arrived at the bower of love, as she called her garret. 'Twas thus our hair became less, and our confectionery for Kalista increased.

When the week had busted on the rock of Saturday night, we used to wander by the brooklet and let the brook wander, too. And Kalista went forth with us. Hand in hand, like the Siamese twinsters, we roamed, and sat on the dewy bank to catch colds in our heads, and luxuriate on the "bank wet with dew!" And we used to recline against a fatherly or motherly elm tree, and squeeze our each other's hands as we rolled our eyes and peeked upward into the blue vault our spirits longed to vault into, but didn't. Oh, this sparking is Heaven in two earthly volumes, with the price-mark omitted! Did you ever spark? If not, advance your works upon a female crinoline-dear, and commence active hostilities to oncet.

Once we sparked Kalista when her mother was looking. The old lady stopped us, 'cause it reminded her of other times, she said. But she didn't keep us stopped. When we wanted to repose our head, Kalista held her lap, and into it we went like an apple. When we wanted a kiss, we told Kalista such was our desire, when she would lean her amber head over upon our forces, and say: "Now, 'Brick,' tea is ready." You jest can gamble we took tea from that little table lots of times, and never asked any one to help put back the plates! Kalista was a zephyr on the kiss. It was pretty near her best holt. Making much was Kalista's charm. When the water would boil, how she did sprinkle meal into the iron—iron—recepteakettle, and shake her locks in glee to see the infant mush bubble and splutter like a fellow kissing a baby with his mouth full of beechnuts.

We courted, sparked, and courted Kalista seventeen long years. She grew from sighs to greater size, and all went merrily as a funeral bell. Kalista's maternal author said we might, and we intended to. We sat on rail fences, end boards to wagon-boxes, piles of pumpkins, heaps of potatoes, door-steps, saw-logs, plough-beams, pine-stumps, where we told our love, and, in anticipation, combed our hair, peeled our potatoes, chopped our hash, rocked our—well, never mind—wore our old clothes, except when we had company, and waxed fat on love and sich. Kalista's father said we might, and there again we had things bagged. We counted our calves, and weighed our pork, and sold our veal, and churned our little mess of butter, and took cur wool to market, and put up our little preserves, and revelled in that future which is so much like an oyster—more shell than meat.

One day a baulky steer slung one of his back hoofs in among the old gent's waistband, and after a series of severe discomfort, the old rooster went hence in February, when we all followed with a march! Kalista was a sensitive plant, measuring fifty-nine inches around afflictions, and so we murdered the steer, and made him into smoked beef. And at supper table, and as we lunched between the heavy courting, we chawed the beef, and thus Kalista and us got satisfaction from the juvenile ox who steered his foot so wickedly.

Then Kalista's mother, who would not partake of the beef, took cold in her head, and went hence. It was autumn—one of the fall months. The mother of our heart's poison—as we family-arly called Kalista—was of an inquiring disposition. She always asked numerous things. She asked the egg man if chickens abided in the shells of the hen-fruit she bought. She wanted to know why rounds were put in ladders crosswise instead of up and down. She wanted to know why pants were made so that a man could not take them off over his head. She said, in her innocence, that an eclipse was caused by a nigger convention between her and the moon! But why the moon fulled rather busted the venerable mother of our Kalista, and she sought to study it out. She read Da boll's Arithmetic, Sands' Spelling-book, Robinson Crusoe, and the La Crosse DEMOCRAT; but she could not get her fork into the reason. The old lady read in an almanac that on a certain night the moon would full. We went to see Kalista that night, to see if our love would full. The old lady determined to watch it and see how a moon fulled, and when it fulled, and what for did it full. Night came, and she wrapped one leg of a pair of red flannel drawers about her head, and when all in the house was still, she emerged into the sitting-room, and in her antique costume. The old lady says: "Brick, your supper is ready!" So we went into the parlor, and kissed the hours away Very fine supper!

The old lady took an almanac, a New York Directory, and a tallow candle out on the back stoop. She anchored in a big chair, and waited to see the moon change its clothes. She looked, and looked, and at last fell asleep for a moment, when, as she said, the *darned thing up and fulled*, and she didn't see it!

She was not an observing female, but she never lost any children. Yet, for all that, the moon worried her—her candle went out. Kalista was left to be her own mother, or do without. Kalista took grief very healthy. She wore mourning, and looked well, as she wept because the jeweller did not get her mourning-pin done in time. She ironed a new cotton handkerchief on the coffin lid, so as to have some use of the furniture ere it was knocked down, and was ready to wedlock then. Kalista was lonesome when her authors were gone, and we should have wedded but for the looks of the thing.

Then there came from the war a journeyman converter, and he offered Kalista all he had, at once. And Kalista, being a lonesome girl, said she would, and she did. And her and the good man went to the carpenter's and ordered a graveyard fence for the loved relatives, and the worker of wood threw in a cradle, and the pair wedded at once, and now Kalista is telling some other delegate that "supper is ready!" And thus another of our hopes is spilled over life's precipice, and we are left to mourn for the candy we gave unto Kalista, who has left us all alone for to die!

CHAPTER XVII.

"Brick" Pomeroy's Evening with Arion.

ARION said come! The C. T. was not enveloped in mystery, but in a white envelope, as all complimentary tickets should be. Grand fancy dress ball. Academy of Music, wit, fashion, shoddy, petroleum, and pretty faces, masked batteries, and such! Did you ever? In this ungodly settlement dwells a charmer. An angelic charmer of the gentler persuasion. She wears hoops. Nineteen springs have fallen over her head. Those dear head, which so erst has reposed on the stalwartest of all arms known in the "Brick" family. Angelic, said you? We went to costumer's. Much display of variety. I went E Pluribus Naturalibus, with mask. Angelic dressed gassy, with white skirt, pink gaiters, corn-colored white kids, red ribbon in muchness, hair widely and vehemently frizzled, and a papier-maché mask, which got mashed over her face, to the great damage of the rouge, who so loves to linger about your lips, you know. We went to the ball. Man with a bear's head and a three-tailed ape took tickets. Angelic and I went in on the roll. Gorgeousness of raiment, and much elevation of head, as though we had each a breast-pin made from crude petroleum; skirmished to the front, advanced masked battery to the stage, flanked a brace of pretty girls with No. 2 gaiters, encamped in a corner of the Arion platform, took Ange's hands in one or two of my hands, and began to grow delirious with pleasure. Ange is a sweet girl, and each returning vernal ripens the love which ripens on her tulips, as pitch oozeth from bark in pine tree. And when it comes to sweetness they do say there is much in I to admire, but it is not as yet generally known. Ange has taken a working interest, and intends developing the property evenings, when the rose sleeps and two lips waken. But why this digression? Yes. Why this di?

We sat. There was an uproariousness of music right and left. There was an army of beauty in the galleries. Yea, there was great beauty in the gals! And at the stage—when we went on the stage—there were boisterous boys on the platform clad in all the queerness of ridiculousness. That ball seemed like a living edition of Babel, or Aldrich's "Baby Bell." It seemed like a modern Congress in full blast, the more so as several innocent ducks, resembling human mourning goods, were to be seen in the scene. We sat and gazed. Ange is good on the gaze. Pretty soon a huge rooster offered his arm to the girl, and she cackleated she'd wander with him. He comes it over me very fowl! I hitched in with a Swiss peasant girl with a milk-pail. Charming little Swiss. Asked her in Swiss, "Wilt prenode?" Answered she in Teuton, "Yah!" Just then the brass band began to toot on, and we walked. Run against soldier. Soldier man scowled. Run against two clowns turning flip-flaps. Nobody hurt. This is quoted! Run against many people. Did not like the jam. No preserves in such jams! Took a lean against private box with girl. Chinese juggler, with a tail on his head like a bovine's narrative, advanced and enraptured my little diary to waltz with him. All right; I hunted for Ange. Just then a tall duck with black leggins, red vest, steel helmet, cross-bars on his back, and huge gloves, waltzed by with my Ange in his arms. I waxed wroth. 'Twas not for that I went to see Arion—his ball. The music was fine. The black knight, who might have been black as night, or a good fellow, waltzed well; but, lordy, how vigorously he voted on the hugging question! Around they went, dodging, bobbing, whirling, darting, and scooting to the right and left, his arms making, in the language of the Psalmist, the waist places glad! Didn't I wish those arms were my arms? Then a herculean Indian grabbed my Ange and whirled her off in the forest of humanity; his arms about her waist, and my heart growing wild with rage—for I can't dance. And that was a funny Indian. He never got tired—at least he did not pant! Oh, dear! If this fun is not original, it is worse—aboriginal. Waltzing is sweet; but darn your hugging—when some one else is hugging your girl! That's what's the matter!

In the jam I lost Ange. I saw everybody and everything else. Dukes and dukesses, nuns and nunesses, kings and kingesses, clowns, Yankees, fat boys, Chinese, Indians, priests, warriors, horse-jockeys, pill-doctors, demijohns, photograph shops, lobsters, pirates, ballet girls, dominos, cowls, and all manner of disguises, but no Ange! Pretty soon, in a fit of desperandum, I froze to a pink skirt with a blue mask- She was dressed like a poet. We, arm in arm, did wonders. I bent my head low, and in gentle tone and manner said:

> Gentle maiden, wilt thou tell
> This stranger where thou dost dwell?
> Give me thy name, and who thou art,
> And rapture bring my beating heart.

And thus gently she spoke: "Nix for-stay."

Good-by, poor Dutchess! I have entangled sleeves with a queen of night, whose pensive brow and heaving breast caused me to think, love her I must. We promenaded. Gently she poised her two hundred pounds avoirdupois on my arm, and now her fat fingers rested on mine. Poetry seized me, and I gently remarked:

> Come to the heart for you now aching—
> Come, raise that deep mask, that I may behold
> The beauty of her I round here am taking,
> And on thee I'll squander a fortune in gold.

And she replied in sweet accents, "Sprachen ye Deitch?"

I gave her up, and made for a gentle nymph, or nymphess, with magic wand, and the zodiac on her apron. Said I, "Wilt walk?" and she wilted. She was fair, else she had not masked. So said I, "Oh! sweet astrologer lady, wilt thou tell the secrets of the stars for me? Tell me, lovely one, if I am to wed a nymph or a nymphess; or if I am to wander through time with no fond soul to cheer me on to high and noble deeds, and no dear hand to comb my hair when tight?" And she said, "Mein Gott in Himmel!"

Verily, verily, I believe all Arion's girls are Dutchesses. Then I made love to a neat little sewing girl, and she raised her mask to show me a mustache and inquire for a chew of tobacco. Sold! And the jam increased. Tried to find Ange. Might as well look for patriotism in a bounty-jumper. Tried to get a supper-room

No go. Tried to get out. Impossible. Never saw such a crowd. Could not have got another person in the building, unless melted and poured in through a funnel. Lost my mask, my ccat-tail, my Ange, and my shape. Got home next morning all out of shape, but bound to see Arion next year, if Congress will pass a law against waltzing with my girl, or for the restoration of the angelic partner of my jammings who was lost in that crowd. I am foot-sore, side-sore, and badly out of shape; but a petroleum vapor bath will bring me to myself, and perhaps bring back my Ange.

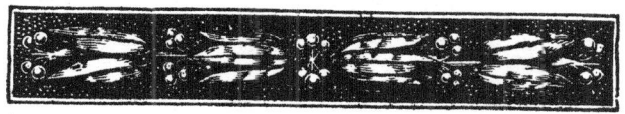

CHAPTER XVIII.

"'Brick' Pomeroy's Experience at Niagara Falls.

IT was two o'clock when I got there.
We went to the International, because I wanted to get inter the national inn. George Colburn, the best and best-looking hotelist in the Northern Confederacy, is at the International, and he is the chief among ten thousand and the one altogether now, three cheers for George.

I took a room. That is, we didn't take it away, for it was too large to carry.

Being in a hurry, we borrowed a candle and

an umbrella and went forth in the night to look at the beauties of nature. Waterfalls are beauties of nature. Selah!

We couldn't see it. That is the Falls. The water tumbled over so fast it hid the falls. Niagara is a great tumbler. There are several tumblers full of it. Next week they are to shut off at 7 P. M., and let on at 6 A. M., except on special occasions. This will save water, and prevent folks from seeing them without paying for them. This is because our colored brother fought so!

We went to our room. The dam roaring out of the window sounded like an army of Fenians or the rushing of many waters. I couldn't sleep, so we raised the window open and looked on the beauties of nature. Bully for nate.

After a while tor wo I fell. That is we fell asleep. What a fall. But not a waterfall!

I dreamed of thee. And there came a rapping upon the chamber. That is to say upon the door thereof. It was made of glass and was full of cider, with lemon rind in it and saccharine about the edges.

"Colburn's comps."

We looked to see what it was, and while looking we lost sight of it. But to memory dear. 'Twas good. We sent for another. It came. Was in need of food. Had read of rinderpest in cattle, so we sent for another glass thing full of cider. It came. 'Twas good. Still hungry. Thought of "fish bait" in pork. Dare not eat pork. Sent for another glass full of cider. The curly-haired cause of the late war smiled. Drank the cider. Felt hungry. Wanted to eat, but the plague in sheep makes mutton dangerous. Couldn't think of mutton, so we tried for another glass of cider. That cider never saw apples, but it must have been made in a cider mill. It made our head think of the way the horse went round. Still hungry. Dare not try sausages. Dogs are poisoned. So we sent for another glass of that, of Colburn. Wanted to know why these things were thus. Still hungry. Thought of ordering fish; but they are poisoned with cocculus indicus. Dare not try fish, for fear some coroner would have to officiate on account of the fish I ate. That is a scaly pun—on a small scale. If the somebody will spear my life, I'll never be caught on that line again by hook or by crook.

I had nine of those beverages in one hour. 'Twas on account of our thirst. Thought it about time to arise and girdle our armor on. Must see Niagara. Unlike gold, the more it falls the better it pleases. Didn't feel hungry. Thought best to get up. Advanced out of bed. Thought I'd take bath. Bath brick are good; so thought a brick bath would be good. Changed our mind. Sat down on edge of bed. Drew on one leg of drawers. Felt queer. The bed had changed sides. Lopped down on bed to hold it straight. Pulled on one boot. Put on vest. Tried to

"Brick's" Experience at Niagara. 159

get night-shirt off after vest was on. Night-shirt beat us. Put on hat. Put on other boot. Tried to pull drawer on over boot. Couldn't. Tried to put on stocking without taking boot off. Couldn't. Rested. Rang for ice-water. Tried to button paper collar to bosom studs. Collar was too short. Tried to put pants on over head, by holding our legs close together. It is an impossibility! Tried to get suspenders under vest without taking vest off. Made our hair pull! Singular how light hair will pull. Tried to tie necktie with one end over our shoulder. Rang for a waiter to find other half of necktie. He found it! Paid waiter a ten-dollar bill by mistake. Tried to brush our teeth with tooth-brush. It had grown so. It was the nail-brush! How our hair pulled! Pulled itself. Had waiter pour ice-water on our head. Had him rub it. Felt better. Niagara Falls are good for headaches! Was four hours in dressing. Took six naps while dressing. Noth ing extra about our wardrobe either. Simple and short, like a Fenian war!

Went to dinner. Lots of people went to dinner. Was not severe on the appetite, but we souped, fished, boiled, baked, roasted, fricasseed, side-dished, entrêed, relished, pastried; was wined, raisined, appled, oranged, figged, and nutted, till our herculean frame felt as full as those head did, after the ninth cock-tail in the A.M. Then a genteel artist, of brunette cast of features, brought us a blue bowl of lemonade. A pint of water, one little piece of lemon about the size of a coat button, and a small towel. A very young towel! Following the example of a countryman at an opposite table, we drank the lemonade, but it was too thin to be exhilarating! Guess it wan't a good day for lemonade. Reckon lemons were skirce!

Never saw so much water for so little "fruit" before. Great watering-place—that is, for lemonade.

Then I went out. We went out. Went out to look at the Falls, that is what we mean. Couldn't see the Falls in the House. Wan't a good day. At least Colburn said so, and he knoweth. Went out with our sweethearts to see the Falls. Wanted to walk. Wanted to rest in that way. Stepped out of the house. Turned the corner.

"*Have a carriage!*"

"No, thank you. Ah, my dear, how beautiful this is—here is the bridge to Goat Island—no goats there now, however. See how the mighty current"—

"*Have a carriage*—drive you all over"—

"No, thank you. The mighty current breaks over the ledges with irresistible force to leap"—

"*I say, mister, will you have a carriage—take you and your*"—

"No, thank you!"

"Leap over the awful precipice to mingle

with the green waters below. Let us walk up this way to obtain a better view of"—

"*Drive you all about the Island for two dollars*"—

"No!"

"The stream as it makes the curve, and leaps along to its death, as 'twere."

"How beautiful!"

"Yes, indeed! We will cross this bridge and go down to Luna Island, where we can hear"—

"*Try my fine garriage, Myneer. It is shust der pest*"—

"No—nix—nein!"

"The roar of the waters as they seem to say"—

"*Shust dake you so goot all over ter falls for a tollar!*"

"No—nein—nix—no—don't want to go over ter falls"—

"Thunder and lightning—excuse me—but what was I going to say?"

"And from here, my dear, we see down the river to the Suspension Bridge—can see the channel worn by the waters, which say as plain as words"—

"*Want a carriage—drive you all over the Island for a dollar!*"

"No, thank you—prefer to stand *right here!*"

"Can speak that the age of the world is greater than"—

"*A description of all the points of interest, only fifty cents!*" says an old man with a little book.

"No, thank you—have been here before!—

"We think for. Let us now walk up the bank, watch the rippling waves by the shore—gather a few flowers—listen to the roar of the wondrous falls—rest 'neath the shade of these wide-spreading branches, and drink in the beauties of this wonderful place. Ah, my dear, here is a little shady bower—the grass carpet is rich, green, and clean—here is a rustic bench—

the sun cannot find us, and side by side sitting we will—

Ragged boy—" Show yer anything you want to see for a quarter!"

"*Go 'way!* Wouldn't give a quarter to see anything we want to see, unless it is you in the dim distance! Get!

" Let care go dancing down the winds, and forget the busy world. Really, this is worth a long journey. And now let us go over to the tower, whose base is washed by the waters which so soon leap down into the foaming abyss, never to return. What fine walks —what beautiful drives, what "—

"*Want a nice carriage—drive you home for half a dollar!*"

"*Yes!* Just wait here till we come back!"

" Can't see it!"

" Splendid views. Across there is Canada. That is the Clifton House, the great Confederate headquarters during the late war. And do you see the crowd of red-coats over there?—the Queen's Own, on the Queen's legs, with the Queen's arms, trembling in fear of the 'blarsted Finnygans,' and all that sort of thing, you know!"

"Ah! they are preparing for evening parade. We hear the drum and fife, we almost hear"—

"*Carriage, sir — drive you back for three dollars!*"

"The command of the officers as they shout"—

"*Carriage, sir—drive you back for half a dollar!*"

"Fall in, men; fall in for evening parade!" (Touch on the shoulder.)

"*Have a carriage, sir — your lady looks wearied!*"

"Yes—*yes*—YES, in GOD's name YES. Two carriages, six carriages—two hundred carriages—a thousand carriages — balm of ten thousand carriages, and we'll ride from Harlem to Hallelujah; from Cape Cod to the irrepressible con flict—from six p. m. to a bottle of claret, if you'll only let us alone. And mind you, if you do not, I'll spew you out of my mouth; I'll tear thee limb from limb; thy mother shall gaze in vain on thy mangled head to discover traces of her whip-cracking infant; I'll make your eyes ache, and the waste places of the earth shall tumble over thy short-haired head like the pictures of Nineveh, as they"—

He's gone! He jumped into his carriage, and is off like a country boy for a doctor, whip in hand, horses on the run, and eye thrown over his shoulder as if struck with fear!

And now, my dear, we will go to the Hermit's Cave—to the cave of the winds—to the ramble—through the brambles—to the curiosity stores—then to the International, and rest on the lawn, or sip a claret punch and be happy.

Yours, at the Falls,

"Brick" Pomeroy.

P. S.—The scared driver told everybody that we are crazy—mad—dangerous—and he offers to bet his vehicle 'gainst a pint of cream that we will jump the Falls in less than forty-eight hours.

CHAPTER XIX.

"Brick" Pomeroy Skateth at the Central Park.

WAS there. Carnival on Central Park Skating Pond. Time—afternoon and evening. Occasion—superabundance of ice. Reason—much skating. Result—great fun. Saw it in the papers. Told Jerusha Mehitible my head ached. J. M. is the sharer of my woes. She didn't read the papers—didn't know of the Carnival. Head grew worse and more worsely. Told J. M. I would go for doctor. Asked her wouldst she if her head ached. Answered she me then, I wouldst. Therefore

I wented. Head didn't ache, however. Went forth. Walked slowly around two corners for fear one wouldn't be enough. Took passage with Oscar. Advanced with Oscar to the Carnival. Marched with vigor to the gate. All right. Then skirmished to left in the direction of Carnival. Verily, verily, big thing. Two bands played music while many girls went forth to skate. Delicate business, that skating! Gazed with admiration on the evoluting crowd who were toying on the bosom of skating pond. Mr. and Mrs. Avenue were there in carriages. The Avenue girls were there. Nice girls. One sweet little dumpling said: "Please give me a hand till I get on the ice?" I gave both hands, and when we reached the glassiness thereof, and she told me she was "on it," how my heart jumped as her heart smiled so sweetly into mine own. J. M. didn't trouble me even in thought, then! Just as I helped my angel with pink skirt and striped hose on the ice, she scooted from me like a bird on wing, so to speak. I gazed and she went. Then I fell back to the reception-room.

One of the Avenue girls, with another one, came in with fun in their eyes, paint on their cheeks, curls on their hair, fancy skating-rings on their bodices, and skates in bags on their arms. I offered to put skates on for them; offer was accepted. Goodness! did you ever hold the foot of an Avenue girl in your lap and gently squeeze the little toes of the little foot in the flurry of getting the skate to fit? Oh! dear, it's fun! And such short skirts, and such pretty Balmoral hose, like little barber-poles of flesh, blood, lightning, and electricity! Helped many skates on to many feet of the Avenue girls. Large family of girls; one of them gave I half a dollar for skating her. Got tired of the exercise, went to office, gave a man half dollar for use of skates; paid boy ten cents to strap them on, and ambled

"I offered to put skates on for them; offer was accept-
[ed]. Goodness! did you ever hold the foot of an avenue
[gi]rl in your lap?"—*Page* 170.

forth to join the whirling throng. Skating is not, in the present year of our Lord, my best forte. But strong heart said "Go it!" Obeyed injunction, and went it. Gracious, but how easy! Just like falling off a log—only a little heavier on the fall. Fine exercise. Many boys and girls mirthed audibly to see me glide rapidly up the pond; and, in trying to dodge two hundred and fifty pounds of skates, in short hoops and red boots, inserted one leg in an air hole. Very moist was that are hole. Got out with agility, and help of a shinny club, and went on. Just as I started, a sweet little chicken, in blue jacket, striped apron, streaked hose, and velvet cap, darted past, and said, "Catch me." Then I urged my mad career on to a close—or toward the animate clothes which was so swiftly on the glide. She dodged, and I dodged. Met a long rooster with eye-glasses, side-whiskers, bobtail coat, fancy skates, limber legs, and a lisp. He yelled, "Take care, fellah!" And we both dodged the same way. I slanted the right skate a point to windward; bobtail anchored. "All right," said I, and passed on. Lost the blue jacket and striped apron in the mêlée. Met timber legs on a limp. He wanted an apology; so did I. We parted in coldness, and he with a contusion on his head.

The music kept playing itself. The crowd kept arriving. Never saw so much style on ice. Blue jackets, red jackets, yellow tunics, green skirts, purple Balmorals, striped hose, red gaiters, pretty ankles, jaunty skating-hats, neat little limbs—O Lordy! but how queer a fellow feels when he feels queerly! And we all skated. Pretty soon, a frolicksome oyster came tearing up the pond, steadying his gray-haired governor. How they glided! And the writer hereafter in their wake.

Pretty girl wanted to take my arm till she learned to strike out. Nice girl—she can have those arms any day. Girl took arm. We sky bugled hither and yon—yon and hither—as the waves dash in on Coney Island. Met a vigorous female scudding before the gale at heavy rate of speed. There was a collision. Pretty girl turned a somersault, and flopped into the arms of a venerable rooster, who stood then and there a looker-on. I anchored on a chilly spot of frigidity, and heard the buttons part company with waistband. The emphatic and limb-fat-ic female had done it.

> With an "ouch" of much anguish,
> And a tear on her nose,
> She squashed and she hid me
> Safe under her clothes.

It might have been fun, but, situated as I was, with those nose of mine flattened on the ice, and two hundred pounds of loveliness, so to speak, on back of an aching head, I couldn't see it. Queer, wasn't it? Preferred the outskirts to the in skirts to skate in. Tried to crawl out. One foot of mine, and two feet of limb-fat-ic female visible beyond the edge of her crinoline. Boy on skates whirled around and yelled, "Hi! hi! Three-legged woman!" Everybody stopped. Crowd came pouring and tumbling in. Rolled over and tried to retreat. Came nigh being smothered. More than twenty girls fell over us. At last I emerged—yes, that is the word—from being where I had not ought to have been. I crawled out from that place of confinement with nose like a potato-blossom, half a hoop-skirt over my head and around my neck. And what work I had getting out; worse than boring for petroleum as I wriggled through a forest of red stockings, variegated circus-tents, skates, and fancy elastics.

Go to where I have been, go see what I have seen, go feel what I have felt, on that Fifth Avenue Skating Pond. Be knocked around and about by the careless crowd, and then tell me if skating carnivals are in reality what they are cracked up to be! All very well for those who keep on their feet, but as for me, give me liberty, or give me—give me—give me a lighter woman to hold me down when the ice is so fearfully and freezingly cold.

It is now morning. I arrived home in a damaged condition. Those hat which adorned that head of mine, by birth, and not by adoption, is gone in. And that are pants be much damaged beyond repair. And our nose is much worried even to this hour. Our cheek is minus a patch of whiskers big enough for a baby's wig, from the fall on the ice. Our watch crystal is in no condition for service. And if ever head ached in this world, head aches now. And J. M., she knows not what is the matter. I told her a Newfoundland dog fell from the ferry-boat, and I became injured in trying to save the life of those dog. J. M. don't love dogs, and says I am a fool. And that immense skating woman who bore down on me so vehemently, I never shall look upon her face again—and I never want to!

CHAPTER XX.

BOSTON BETSEY'S "BRICK," OR "BRICK'S" BETSEY.

FOUND her in Boston. Betsey Jerusha Jones—in three volumes illustrated. I thirsted for intellect. I hungered for beauty. I ached for charms. I required a gentle being with a mind like horse billiards to guide me through this vale of steers. I went to Boston to find my love. I found her. She was a school teacher, who drew seven dollars a month for spanking the rule of three into the vulgar fractions confided to her charge, and for adding accomplishments as 'twere to the result of others' multiplication! Figuratively speak-

ing. After school was disbanded for the day, we walked out to the beach. Birch by day and the beach by night.

My love was beautiful. She was of the New England type. She was *pure*-itanical. Thus worshipped I her, the most beautifulest ant in the sugar bowl.

And she made both ends meet by skinning eels. She was a most exalted and triumphant eel skinnist. The Massachusetts girls teach schools and skin eels for the market. Said I, "Betsey, if it's not a-skin too much, let me go out with thee and aid in thy toils, and see thee divest eel of cuticle. She said, yea. I went. She had a hooked nose. She had three hoops—at regular intervals. She was Massachusetts schoolmarm. She was old maid. She understood all of Daboll but the multiplication. She had never been on the multiply! Oh, no! And she could skin eels faster than the devil could catch a fiddler.

By the beach we sat. She skinned eels for the net proceeds. We talked of love and sich. She listened to my tale. She felt the moving of my plea; the burning eloquence thereof,—so called. Said I—

"Oh! Betsey, seein' its yeou, I love yeou, I sweow. I wouldst be thine. I would share thy cot, and

> 'Dream I sleep with thee, love.'

Wouldst be mine? I am a stranger, Betsey. I am not aged, but on the contrary, am agile as those eel. I will offer thee all I have. I would be thus to thee. I would crawl out of myself as those eel crawls out of his undershirt in thy hands, and be thine onlyest."

She took up another eel.

"Oh! Betsey," said I, as I laid partly on the grass, partly in the lap of Betsey, with the slickery tails of her eels tickling my nose—"were you ever caressted by mortal?" She said, no, and looked sidewise.

She took another eel.

I then caressted her. Said she, "Praise the Lord, but that is the first kiss ever mortal man gave me." I asked her if she liked it? She said it war better nor spanking a young un, or skinnin a big eel. She said she liked school-teaching. It was better than a gymnasium. She said kissing was better than skinning eels. When a Massachusetts girl says that, you may, with the lambs on the hills, gamble that she liketh it with vehement muchness.

The pale moon slid along overhead just as easy! It seemed to skin itself from under the fleecy clouds, as those eels skinned themselves from the fingers of my Betsey Jerusha. It set me to thinking she was something heavenly like the moon. Only she was a little plumper. It was a new moon Newer than Betsey, and a little slimmer. I-conversed with Betsey. She had a little knife like a shoe knife. I would have thought her a shoemaker if she had carried a cobbler's kitten and a waxed end. But she didn't. She skinned eels, chawed spruce gum, and talked love. Said she—

"What is your name?"

Asked we, "The reverberating cognomen to which we respond?"

Said she, "Yes."

Said we, "'Brick' Pomeroy."

Then she asked us of our Western home. She wanted to know what State Illinois was in, and if Wisconsin was in the First or Second Ward of La Crosse. And she wanted to know if we had young ones in the West. We told her not many, yet! Then she wanted to know if the Mississippi river had eels in it. We told her, nay. And she wanted to know if the people out in that barbarous region wore clothes every day, or only when they went sparking. And she wanted to know how far it was from where we lived to a house. And she wanted to know if they spanked or ferruled youngsters in schools, and if we had schools. And she wanted to know if women dressed in bearskins or tilting hoops, which we suppose are all the same! And she wanted to know if we had newspapers, and could read and write, and had ever heard of Anna Dickinson. And she wanted to know if it was not terrible living so far from Boston!

Then I caressted her and kissed her so sweetly. And she twined the eel skins in a garland and wreathed them about our neck as she sat there in maiden meditation fancy free, like a box of No. 11 boots. Then we said—

"Oh! Betsey Jerusha, thou hast spokenest with wisdom. I will converse with thee, elastic nymph. I am a barbarian. We are all barbarians in the West. I am an ignorant but well-meaning whelp. We are all ditto in the West. I wear bearskins in the West—we all ditto in that country. We have no houses, but live intently without them as 'twere. We have no carriages for either male or female, so called

But I can love thee. I can hold thee to mine own. I will surround thee with all the luxuries we have in that land of darkness, for the sun never rises in the West!"

Said Betsey, as she playfully slung the hide off from another conquered eel, "*Deu tell!*"

I wanted information, and thus we dialogued:

"My Betsey Jerusha, hast much of parents?"

"Yes, Brickuel, I have two parents and four ante-parents."

"What diddest they do?"

"My ma taught school and skinned eels, and my father was an eel-catcher and a silver-tongued politician."

"How many boys canst spank in a day?"

"I have spanked twenty-seven in an hour, and it wan't a good hour for spankin, either!"

"And eels! How many eels canst thou peel in a day. Tell me, thou educator of the world?"

"Well, now, that is a pretty right smart of a

question! I guess I can skin six a minute. I skin 'em and sling 'em over my shoulder into that are tub, and kin keep one in the air all the time, and I ain't much of a skinnist, nuther!"

"Does it hurt the eel?"

"Why, of course it kills the eel! But that is his fault. If he'd had his skin put on t'other side out 'twouldn't hurt 'm any! 'Twould have slid off itself? It's our doctrine in New England to have things conform to our notions, even if the eels we skin don't like it. You see this is the hub; and the eels have no rights that we, the skinners, are bound to respect!" and into the air she playfully tossed another yard of subdued, quivering agony!

Says us—

"Do you skin 'em for fun or for profit?"

Betsey said it was for both. There was money in it, and it was fun to see them squirm, for they had no business to be eels, and to come to New

England in the spring and fall for what they wanted. And thus Betsey taught me to love. Gentle, Christianized Betsey!

And I kissed her. And I hugged her there, then. And I told her she should be happy. And that she should have eels to skin forever. That I'd have 'em made on purpose! Then she smiled and said she'd be mine, so called, if I'd agree to find her in eels; to find young ones for her to spank; to let her come once a year to hear the big organ and rock her baby in the cradle of liberty; to let her kiss every nigger she saw; to let her spend half her time in peddling tracts and making flannel shirts for babies in Africa, and would do my best to extend the blessed gospel and the likeness of Ben. Butler in the benighted region beyond the hub.

I consented to all she wanted of me except the nigger. On that I was firrum. So was Betsey. She said "nigger, or single blessedness." She said they were her pets. I told her I was a

Democrat. Oh, gracious! She straightened up till her corsets snapped like a pistol! I thought she had gone off! But she hadn't. She was there yet. Said she, as she scrunched an eel in her hand, and waved her peeling machine over her head:

"You a Democrat! Marry a Democrat? Go 'way! Git eout! Don't tech me! Oh, you great, ugly Western man! Take your arm away from around my intellectual breast! Oh! you great, ugly, Western man! I'd skin you like an eel! Oh, *git eout!* Rise your hoary locks from that ere lap! I'll take my eels and fly from your advances! Marry a Democrat? I'm no such woman! Oh! you great, big, red-whiskered, gray-headed, savage, unrefined, uncultivated, uneddicated, big, nasty man! How dare you talk to me? I'd die first, and then I wouldn't!"

And she done as Joseph did in the night, and went off into Egypt, leaving me in a bed of eel-skins. And now I'm a gone nutmeg, a busted what-do-you-call-it. I've lost my Betsey Jerusha, and must live in the West, beyond the eels and school-marm charms of her I so adored, for us of the West are not of the eel-ite.

Thine, unskinned,
"BRICK" POMEROY.

CHAPTER XXI.

How to Buy Oil Lands.

NEEDEEP, MUD COUNTY, VA.,
March 20, 1865.

ORD bless you, but the rain did come down, and the mud did come up, and at times the current of conversation would be stopped by a vehement damn, as spatterrings of Virginia mud would be thrown halfway down a poor fellow's throat, as our party single filed along, through the miry clay on toward the oil region.

Oil on the brain! How are you, "Peter

Oleum?" Right smart—glad for to hear you are able to get out!

The city of New York, or the settlement of ungodliness, differs a whole mess from the oil region. If you are unbelievers and not disposed to take stock in this assertion, come ye out and try it. Risk your life. Purchase mourning for your friends, if your ticket is by the Camden and Amboy line of coffins. Eat dog sausage and benevolent hash at railroad eating-houses; force muddy juice of burnt rye and yellow beans down your throat, and think it is coffee; spear chunks of fat pork as they swim round in an earthen basin filled with hot lard oozing out of the dirty cracks thereof; sleep on mud floors with hogskin saddle for pillow; drink corn whiskey so new that you can actually feel the corn silk in it, as, like a drunken torchlight procession, it winds down the throat; eat bread heavy enough to make into nail hammers, and curse the country because fine tooth combs cannot be purchased at the groceries. I should say New York differed from the oil regions, yet it is real fun to skirmish about here, looking for the main chance, and prospecting for indications of the great fluid.

When I made up my mind to visit the oil regions, a little note was sent to my Ann Jane, telling her that soon after dark began to dawn on all things here below, she would hear the door-bell. The door-bell meant me. Ann Jane received the letter, and got herself up in style. There may be sweeter girls than her, but she will do. Oh, yes, she will, and I know it. Regardless of taste or expense was my toilet made. Like a night-blooming cereus looked I. Active as an ant on a hot griddle I advanced up the steps to her brown-stone front, rang the bell, and went in. We met the usual way—so the report said. Talk about new mown hay, sweet cream, a love of a bonnet, or a new baby, that dear Ann Jane is so much sweeter than all them, it is a wonder they existeth.

We sat on the sofa. Her father was a wealthy man; but had sold short that day, and was not extensively well. Economy is a good thing. Ann Jane and I sat on the sofa. We turned the gas down low for economy. I had on patent leather boots, with red tops and yellow silk straps, rather elegant pants, and a large bunch of other clothes, with a greatness of candy in pockets. We talked—Ann Jane is a good conversationer. I told her that oil was what oiled me. In childhood's balmy days aunty always gave me oil, with happiest effect, and I must have more. Ann Jane coincided. We ate up the candy, which seemed to grow weary of its perpetual sweetness, as the two lips of my student in economy rewarded me from time to time with the sweetest—never mind though, now.

I started. With clarion notes the roosters escorted me to the cars. Like a man going to his grave, I entered cars, first looking to the priming of my life and accident insurance policy.

How to Buy Oil Lands. 191

And such a whole parcel of things as I had to travel with! Peruse the list, brave volunteers of Peter!

Black bag for things,	. 1	Slippers for feet, . . .	2
Comb for the hair, . .	1	White vest for parties, .	1
Brush for the hair, . .	1	Patent-leather boots for	
Shirts for the body, . many		style, ...	2
Toothpicks for the teeth, ... several		Kid gloves for hand, .	2
		Late novels, ...	6
Handkerchiefs to use, .	1	Several other things, . .	1
Perfumery to smell, .	lots		

Not much baggage, but considerable what there was of it. The conductors on the railroads kindly allowed us to ride in safety, greatly to the disappointment of many people.

We all arrived in Virginia to find the sacred soil thereof dotted with oil hunters. After a fine sleep on the floor, waiting for the bed to grow empty, morning broke. After breakfast, mounted on much horse, I started for oil regions. Horses in Virginia are horses.

I know they are not oxen, for of horns they have none, and their tails grow bushy. They are fast animals. Seated on top of one of them, I had no trouble in making two miles an hour toward a corn crib. Once, I actually passed a yoke of old oxen, hauling a little old man, a fat old woman, a bundle of corn stalks, and jug of corn whiskey, on an old bob sled. Fact! Virginia horses deserve premiums, for what they lack in legs they make up in ribs. Some of them have two eyes, and sometimes may see a currycomb—doubtful if they ever feel one, however. And the saddles! they give tender recollections which even now stir up the feelings! They don't some steal horses in Virginia as much as in other States. In fact, it would be a dangerous job if the pursuer happened to travel on foot. And this is my opinion of Virginia horses! Selah.

There are many things oil will buy, so we

wanted a whole mess of it. In order to make a good impression before getting on the back of the fleet steed, whose apt name was "Bony," so the livery delegate said, I took advantage of the crowd, and with camphor, ice, and cologne, made myself handsome to the smell, with a flask (in which to bring back samples of oil), I "elevated" myself to the new position, and set gently forth. The horse had a gait; a plain, austere, radical gait enough to bring a hoss-tear from his rider.

Bravely I struck out. Through the mud of Western Virginia went I like the solitary horseman with several other mounted roosters going up a long hill; over the tumble in bridges; through the tumble in bridges; wading the very wet creeks; sticking fast in the affectionate mud; past houses resembling the first efforts of a school-boy at architecture on a slate. I smelt of the mud; tasted the water; felt of the rocks; soaked my handkerchief in the creek; looked at the bony legs of my bony horse to see if they were greasy from his boring the mud with half-shoed hoofs; asked many men if oil did abound there or thereabouts; propounded questions to many women, and patted a considerable of Virginia children on the head, and inquired for oil territory, indications and developments.

At last, after the sun had concluded to retire, and after I had suffered on the top of that horse for seven hours, and ridden, if you call it riding, eleven miles as the chap said, back to Widow Gartan's barn, I rode up to a log mansion built out-doors against a big mud chimney. The horse stopped very easy; in fact, stopping was his best gait. I made friends with five dogs and rapped on the open door.

"Come in," says a man.

"Thank you," says I.

"Yes, come in," said a woman.

"Ah! yes, thank you," said I.

"Get out," said the man.

"Get out," said the woman.

The five dogs left-wheeled, and got out at a very vehement double slow.

"Good year for dogs. Nicest lot of dogs I have seen.

"Right smart dogs, stranger," said the old man.

"Right smart dogs," said the old woman.

I took a chair, a very fine one, made of an old nail keg, and looked. If the house had one more room, there would have been two rooms in it. The man was a quaint old rooster, well out of his pants, all around and at each end. His head was high, and his forehead so broad, that it ran clear to the nape of his neck. He had grown clear through his hair, and was heavy on smoking native tobacco in a red clay pipe.

There was more of his wife than of him, by a wheelbarrow full. He was slim. She did not slim a bit. He was tall. She had never talled much. His arms were long. And it was a good thing, for he never could have hugged his wife alone, had they not been long. Her arms were short. She did not need long arms to hug him. O Nature, how kind you are in such cases! And she had such short taper toes—ten of them all together; and there was no squeak to her footsteps as she glided about the room like a thing much of life. When he spoke, she spoke; when he talked, she always followed suit, playing the left bower on his right. She clinched his conversation by repeating it. She varnished his talk by endorsing it. She walked the house and always endorsed what the major said. Every man in Virginia is an officer. I always salute a man as colonel in that country. Other folks say "Mister." "Mister" is too thin, and folks say the man who calls other folks plain "Mister" is from Vermont!

Stretching legs before a singing fire, we had

the following conversation, the better half being always on hand to clinch things.

"Can I get to stay here to night?"

"Reckon not, unless your hoss ken stand it outside and go hungry."

"No corn?"

"Not a corn, stranger. The home guard took my corn."

"Any oil about here?"

"Right on this farm."

"Ah! how much land have you here?"

"Well, there is a right smart of land. You see I own a lot here, and my old Aunt Elizabeth, who had a hoss run away with her five years ago when she was riding down to the court-house to see the sheriff who was one of the dodrottedest meanest men that ever got elected into office, which he never would have done if Bill Mason, who run agin him, had not had a power of money and more friends—for Bill's father owned the tavern on the forks, and him and Tom Cowler were thick as bees ever since Bob Jones had the scrimmage with Hank Jenks about the old blind mare which Hank sold to Tom's father, and which was stolen by some cussed thief the night of the law-suit between——

"Get out!" to a red dog which was coming in the door.

"Get out?" yelled the old woman, and out went the dog.

"How much land did you say you had here, Colonel?"

"Oh, right smart, altogether. There was five hundred acres on the Spring farm; but the old man sold it off the range to Colonel Black the spring the colonel's wife died—thanks to the inchronicus disease which seemed to drive her into consumption even after the Colonel had got her three dozen bottles of Cod's liver oil in Baltimore, which I don't believe would cure a dog, and I don't care what ailed him; and all the neighbors say so, except Squair Jacobs, who says he had a niece who had a right smart of larning, and drove a school when she warn't but rising onto nineteen years in the log school-house with the window out, just as you pass by where lame Dick has got up a blacksmith shop where he will shoe a horse in less than no time——"

"Yes, I know, Dick. And how many acres have you now?"

"Oh, there is right smart of land, and I don't care to sell it now, for John is off fighting into the army, and me and the old woman have all we can do to make a living here, and have to work every day, except once in a while we get a jug of the creature and have a rest, but for which—

"Get out, you pesky brute," said the old man.

"Get out, you nasty hound," said the old woman as she aimed a wooden poker at a brindle dog, who was helping himself to a piece of corn-bread. The dog got out!

"Well, Colonel, what are the chances for finding oil on the property about here?"

"Oh, right smart, I reckon. You see, down on the bottom, long in the summer, there is the peculiarist smell, and I allers knowed it was something; and now I know it is oil, for Bob Spears sold his farm on the run above here, and the men what bores it now has got two wells onto the lower lot, and Squire Barnard says the show is jest as good on my farm as on Spears' farm; and the squire is right powerful on larnin', and went to school twenty years ago, when he was a boy, and sparkin' Dorothy Slawson, whose father was killed in the row he had with Bill Ransom, after he shot Bill's red heifer."

'What do you call your land worth, Colonel? cash down soon as you can make out the papers."

"Well, stranger, it wants a right power of money to get this ere land now, for me and the old woman has got seven hundred and nineteen acres here, and as there can be put ten wells on each acre, and each well will give a hundred barrels of oil, and as oil is worth $15 a barrel, I am figuring up how much me and the old woman will be worth, and if you want the farm for what it figures up for a year and a half or two years, just say the word, and me and the old woman will sell it to you for half what it's worth, and you can have the house to live in, and me and the old woman will take the dogs."

"Yes, me and the old man will take the dogs, for they are right smart dogs," said the old woman.

"Well, let's see, Colonel. Seven hundred and nineteen acres; ten wells to the acre; seven thousand one hundred and ninety wells—one hundred barrels to a well—seven hundred and nineteen thousand barrels—fifteen dollars a barrel—makes ten million seven hundred and eighty-five thousand dollars, no cents. I'll take the property, Colonel."

"Now, stranger, you figger so fast—all them fellers what figgers in their heads kinder beats me somehow—that I am fear'd you ain't right;

and agin, you didn't figger it but for one year, and the land is worth right smart more than that; but the sums that me and the old woman do, don't come out alike all the time, so I'll have Squire Barnard figger it for me, being as you're a stranger; and if he figgers it as you do, and you will make it for two years, me and the old woman will see about it."

"Yes, we'll see about it," said the consort.

"Well, Colonel, have you any of your figuring (noticing an old slate, covered with figures, hanging on a nail drove in a jamb), that I could look it over and see how it compares with mine?"

"Oh, yes, me and the old woman don't do nothing in the day times but figger now, and you jest run your eye over this (handing me the slate), and see how it compares with your brains."

I took the slate, which was all right, except a corner was gone, and found where he had "figgered" with a piece of soft stone in lieu of a pencil, as follows:

119
 10
───
009
119
───
1199
  15
────
11995
 5575
─────
68745
  100
─────
68745
68745
68745
──────
662.695
    119
───────
17841205
 6621695
 6621695
─────────
1245327655

His figures were somewhat "incoherent," not to say high, so I bade the old couple good-day, mounted that horse, and skirmished on to the next stopping-place.

CHAPTER XXII.

A Chicken Suit.

MONDAY forenoon there came off before Police Judge Hubbard, in La Crosse, another law suit, the particulars of which are as follows:

Reinhardt Hendricks, on the 17th of September, 1866, brought suit against "Brick" Pomeroy, to recover pay for two roosters shot by the defendant with a revolver, the chickens belonging to the plaintiff, to the value of fifty cents each. Through the kindness of the judge the case has been adjourned from week to week till the return of the defendant from an electioneering tour in Indiana. This morning the case came off, Ex-Mayor Hon. James I. Lyndes being the counsel for the prosecution, the defendant appearing in his own behalf.

The court-room was crowded, for the idea of trying an editor for stealing or shooting chickens was a novelty. The plaintiff brought in his bill, swore to its correctness, testified that he owned the chickens, that they were raised by a hen belonging to him, that he saw the defendant shoot them, that he had repeatedly asked the defendant to settle for them, and failing to get pay or satisfaction, he was compelled to bring suit, and asked for judgment of one dollar, and costs.

The defendant admitted shooting the chickens, and proved by four reliable witnesses the following facts:

In April, 1866, the defendant owned a fast-running trick mare, "Kitty," which animal was kept in a stable hired by him, and cared for by one of his employés. Through a little hole in the barn or stable the plaintiff's hens would fly in and eat oats intended for the mare "Kitty," and on the approach of any one would fly out. In an old barrel in the stable, one of the hens, a black one, made her nest, laid thirteen eggs therein, and proceeded to raise a family. When the hen got ready to set, the defendant instructed the boy who took care of his mare to go down town, purchase thirteen eggs of J. W. Robinson & Co., grocers, and put them in the nest, first removing the other eggs. The boy did so, as was proved. He then personally drove the hen out of the stable a dozen times or more—he tried to make her leave—she would not, but proceeded to incubate his eggs, duly bought and paid for, without his consent, leave, or license, after repeated efforts on his part and by his agents to have her vacate his premises. And, further, when the hen had hatched the eggs, she ran away with his chickens, eleven in number, two eggs not producing chickens.. To her services he brought an offset, the use of stable and board bill in the shape of oats—he charged her with the two eggs she spoiled, and demanded judgment for the balance of the flock, nine in number, at fifty cents each. And, besides, he proved that the chickens did not belong to that hen, as she was black, while the chickens were red or speckled! Hendricks has sued all his neighbors for some little trifling matter half-a-dozen times each during the past two years.

After a patient hearing, the judge decided that there was no cause of action, and that the defendant was entitled to the other nine chickens, and the plaintiff must pay the costs of the suit, amounting to seventeen dollars and thirty-seven and a half cents.

CHAPTER XXIII.

As a Pic-Nic-ist.

S a Pic-Nic-ist I have reached!
It was a calm, hot morning, about the half of July, 1867. The weather was all that could be desired with forty-seven degrees plus. I may say it was in a melting mood, with several meltings over. And why not, when such is thus?

Eulelia Jane said it was too hot to keep cool, and that we must go to a Pic-Nic for the benefit of the church. I asked Eulelia, if it was for the benefit of the church, why go forth when it was so d—readfully hot. Said Eulelia, "Don't swear," and I sweared not any. Then she said it was to teach us that hot places should be shunned. And so we went.

I am much fond of them—I mean Pic-Nics. Base-ball is good for exercise, but nothing compared to Pic-Nic. It is a good way to have cheap amusement—and much of it—at light expense. Eulelia is a sickly plant. She needs the fresh air. Being a stout cherub, I often go out with her to get a little air.

After breakfast we started for the Pic-Nic—Eulelia Jane and I. The sun was suffused with blushes, and Eulelia Jane was

> Beautiful as a flutterby,
> And none could compare
> With my pretty little charmer
> And her rich, wavy hair.

I knew the sun was in love with my fragile pet, else why those burning glances as we passed? Eulelia Jane carried a parasol and hymn-book. The Pic-Nic was on church account. I was proud as the first roasting ear of this loveliness. How my heart and things warmed to her as we went forth. We were going to a Pic-Nic. I took along a few little things to use at the Pic-Nic. Merely a few little things that Eulelia Jane might want. There was not much, as all the men took a little something. All I had to take was Eulelia's poodle and a dog to guard it, a few eatables, and implements to be used for the Pic-Nic; two hams, a case of crackers, ten loaves of bread, nine bottles of catsup, sixteen boxes of sardines, seven custard pies, a jug of cold coffee, a box of lemons, ninety-three cucumbers, a quart of pepper-sauce, a box of raisins, nuts, and candy; some cold tongue, a block of ice, some few chunks of dried beef, a basket of champagne, an axe, two hatchets, crowbar, spade, rope ladder, a Sunday-school library of books, fifty palm-leaf fans, a pew-cushion to keep Eulelia from taking cold, two hundred feet of rope for a swing, keg of spikes, water-pails, and other articles of bigotry and "virtue," including a marble-top table, and fixings for an amateur base-ball game.

Did I say Eulelia was lovely? Yessy, yessy! She was sweeter than any other woman, and there was more of her. She was an only child! But she was much! It is good to have something to lean against. So she said we would go forth to Pic-Nic. So everybody went. That is why we had a good time.

It is only four miles to the sylvan grotto where rural felicity had secreted himself. Rural felicity! Them is the feller!

Eulelia went first, and I followed her with the things. I have been told that we wanted for nothing. But we did. I wanted a horse to aid me in toting things. It was a hot day, or there would have been no need of Pic-Nic. We walked four miles, Eulelia ahead, and I carrying and drawing the things. Eulelia is playful. She got off a pun at which all the others smiled severely. She said I was good at drawing! I should say so. So would any one be who had my load.

We went to the top of a high hill to get a breeze! Eulelia said it would be cooler there. That was what we sought, and perspired because we found it not. It was a high hill. On the brink of a precipice. There was one tree there. The breeze, therefore, had a fair sweep. At ten o'clock we reached the summit. As an activitest I bore good repute. Two miles distant, in the woods, at the foot of the hill, was a cool spring. Being a nice, good-natured, active, little man, I was sent for water. Eulelia said I could go just as well as not. She takes pride in my agility. I did not hear the suggestion. Eulelia lifted up her voice. I heard and went. No gentleman will contradict his wife!

Them other fellers said they would fix things, and I might rest by going for water. I went down the hill at the peril and danger of my life

—what was left. And I had such a pleasant time getting back. Two pails full of water—not a dry joke, else why this perspiration? I enjoyed this rise in the world, and thanked Eulelia for the same.

When I returned with water they had fixed things. They were seated on the grass, under the tree. The claret was no more. The ice lay weeping in the sun. Eulelia said it made it seem cooler! And she said if the ice melted I would go back for more. Sagacious sylph! Never contradict your wife!

Pretty soon we had dinner. Eulelia said I could set lunch better than any other man. The other fellers said so. They sat in the shade, smashing flies, while I spread for lunch. The marble-top table came handy.

I asked one of the gentlemen if he would open the sardines and cut the lemons. He was a gentleman, and remarked—

"I'll see you in —— first!"

He was a playful duck. I opened the sardines —all but him! The folks said I was a nice man, so kind and agreeable!

We had a fine dinner. I had what was left. Then Eulelia proposed that we have a swing erected.

Being a spry man, I had to climb a tree to adjust the ropes. It wan't the distance up, but it was the roughness—very hard on wearing apparel. At last I fixed the ropes. The swing was too low. It dragged on the ground.

Being a man of muscle, and expert in the use of pickaxe, I had to grub a trench. Eulelia said I could do it quicker than any other man, and— no gentleman will contradict his wife!

I picked and shoveled for three hours, and at last removed enough rocks to start the swing. We had a good time. It is fun to swing.

Trenching is good. My trench was wide and deep, that the hoops might clear. Eulelia she tried it. Four of us steadied her into the contrivance. We pulled her back, like the cock to an old musket, and then let her go. She went through the air like a humming-bird—like a fairy. I began singing—

"See! oh, see my flower!"

When there was a screech! The limb to which the rope was fastened failed to keep up. It lacked backbone! It let down, and Eulelia was fast in the trench. Being very modest, she would allow no one but me to help her out! I worked two hours enlarging the trench, and at last rescued her.

I wanted her to try it again, but she smiled sweetly, and said one plateful was enough. Being active, I had to run down hill and back to the city for arnica liniment. Eulelia wanted it. I didn't ask her what for. It was none of my business. Husbands, obey your wives!

Exercise is good. I had enough that day. I got this flower and that flower. I climbed

As a Pic-Nic-ist. 217

to the tops of trees like a red squirrel after something. I was let down the precipice by a rope to hunt for eagles' nests. I was sent after water, ice, and such things, and seriously hurt my pants in the bird's-nest business.

But we had a delightful time. Such a cool, pleasant time! Eulelia drank so much lemonade she was sick. So I drew her to the edge of the precipice in the little wagon I had dragged along, and let the breezes fan her brow.

The others couldn't wait, and they went. Eulelia wanted to see the moon rise. She said it would be nice to look down and see it come up. So she sent me home with the things, and told me to hurry back for her as soon as I could, like a dear little man. Then she sat on the edge of the rock, her feet pointing to the hunting-grounds beyond La Crosse. In one hand she held her parasol, and in the other her book, while her pretty poodle snoozed in her lap.

Eulelia was happy—I knew it. The sun was sinking in the West. The gnats and mosquitoes were tuning their lyres and biting Eulelia's nose, but she was bound to see the moon rise. Nothing like a novelty.

As I gayly swore my way down the rocky steep, I saw a picture.

It was Eulelia on a rock, singing—

"I want to be an Angel!"

Such a day of sport! Let all who want fun go to a pic-nic.

Agilitiously Thine,

"Brick" Pomeroy.

CHAPTER XXIV.

"Brick" and the School-Marms.

JUST full of them!

Oh, son of mortal parents! did you ever? Only think—half a regiment of school-marms on a visit to La Crosse! Who cares for business, for newspapers, for meals or lodging, wealth, playthings, or raiment; for are not the school-marms here on a visit to stay with and bless us three days—to tantalize us with their bright eyes, pretty faces, funny waterfalls, neat dresses, ripe lips, peachy cheeks, gentle manners—and—and—

"Oh I want to be an angel,
And with a angel stand,
Or sit along with school-marms,
And hold 'em by the hand!"

If we go to the post-office, they are there!

If we go to the bank, they are there!

If we wander forth to look for local items, behold, fifteen school-marms are there!

If we fly to the bluffs, on our running horse, behold, they are there, looking for roses, and posies, to hold up to their noses!

If we wander forth where there is a crowd of youngsters playing with kites, behold more than a multitude of school-marms are there, like spiders waiting to pounce on their prey!

Go where we will, there are school-marms, and nine-tenths of our citizens are going crazy. Sweethearts here residing tremble when their lovers pause to look; married ladies look their prettiest to retain their loves; and all the beardless boys in town are wishing they were a

"Oh! I want to be an angel, and with a angel stand, or
[s]t along with schoolmarms, and hold 'em by the hand!"—
[P]age 220.

little older! It's the school-marms. And four fifths of them are Democrats, and things of beauty are joys forever. Selah!

> I'd like to be a school-marm—
> And wouldn't I if I could?
> It's you love, they love, I love,
> How they make us all feel good!

Oh, Father of our Country! Beloved Washington! we look up to that smiling face so sadly beaming, and think how much you missed by not being at La Crosse! And the noble patriots of the revolution, with their blood-stained banners, and their elastic step, and their pretty balmorals——

Confound it, here we are on the school-marms!

And where was Clay, and Webster, and Horace Greeley, and the founders of the Roman Empire? They lived as do we, but they saw not the sights our eyesight has this day sighted—school-marms by the multitude. The names we have quoted all belonged to men who have lived in history, but are now dead! They had friends, and they saw—such bright eyes and lips, just good enough for even the editors of the La Crosse DEMOCRAT to taste, and the prettiest mouth, and the most charming *naïveté*, and the bewildering effect of——

Here we are, on the school-marms again!

The Constitution expressly says that taxation shall be equal—that the rights of States shall never be wrested from them—and that a people who have suffered long from evils unmentionable, shall have new unmentionables—and our white vest and well-shaved face, and a clean white handkerchief—then bring our new boots and switch-cane, that we may just step out a few moments——

Confound the school-marms! How can we write on politics now?

But to resume our seat at the desk. Here is a letter advising us to speak more boldly for repudiation. Well do we know that the war debt is a burden imposed for no good, but the people are willing dupes, running here, and— there goes four more school-marms, and I'd give just forty dollars in gold if that one with the witching eyes and dark hair was my sweetheart, when I'd

> Wander forth by moonlight
> Along with that school-marm,
> And, golly, how I'd fight
> To shelter her from harm!

Now, how can a man write editorials to-day? If we open a letter, there is a school-marm with red lips, saying plain as possible, "Don't!"

And if we would make change in settling for something, there is, in the cash-box, another school-marm, with the sweetest mouth, seeming to say "Do." And you bet—no, you needn't bet— you'd lose!

And if we tear the wrapper from one of our

exchanges, behold we see nothing but a school-marm—

> Gay as a butterfly,
> And none can compare
> With one little school-marm
> Who sat right over there!

Close the office — shut the doors — stop the presses, open no more mails, for the school-marms are here! Let business go to the dogs, and let everybody have a rest, that we may gaze on half a regiment of girls, most of them handsome. Golly! Don't we sigh for the good old days, when we used to stay after school to sweep the school-house and kiss our teacher.

Once	*	*	*	*	*	*	remember
*	*	*	*	*	*	*	pretty Jane
Spelling-book	*	*	*	*	*	*	December
*	*	*	*	*	*	*	Once again!

Go it, boys! School-marms! *take 'em on the fly!*

"Brick" and the School-Marms.

Just think of it—half a regiment of handsome girls in La Crosse—all visitors—all the observed of all observers—all out to Convention. How many a heart will follow them home. They will be pillars of smoke by day and waterfalls of fire by night to lead our La Crosse boys over the country from home bases to other fields.

"Tell the" schcol-marms all around you not to do it. Tell them not to take prisoners the ones who never saw such beings of beauty before.

Egad, how I'd like to be school-marm!

> I'd like to be a school-marm,
> And with the school-marms stand,
> With a bad boy over a barrel
> And a spanker in my hand.

And when the exercises were over, how the little younkeys would run home, singing—

> "I would not live forever,
> I ask not to stay

> Where an out-of-patience school-marm
> Does things in that way!"

Wouldn't it be fine to go to some of these school-marms' temples and be set with the girls, and kept after school! Some of them would witchety-switchety our little legs, and spank our little ears, and stand us on little dunce-blocks—oh, no!

> "High over the hill-tops resounding,
> Come the notes of deeds begun!
> 'Come out, Bill Jones, and take your pounding,
> For I saw you tickling Julia Plum.'
> So Bill comes out, his shirt and breeches
> Well shaken by his trembling form,
> And the school-marm larrups him with switches,
> Till his resting-place is awful warm!"

You bet! "Now, Bill Jones, go to your seat, and keep your fingers away from Julia's ribs!" "Please, school-marm, may I go out?" "Hold your hush, what are you 'bout? What you want to go for?" "Please, ma'am, I can't tell." "Then keep your feet together, while you spell!"

We'd love 'em—we'd take 'em apples, candy, bouquets, newspapers with love stories in, and we'd kiss them if they'd let us. Don't say no—

"Teach not thy lips such scorn, *for it was made*
For kissing, lady, not for such contempt."

And then all the other boys! wouldn't they be jealous? Wouldn't the green one-eyed lobsters gnash their teeth and refuse to learn their lessons?

"Hence, jealousy; thou fatal, lying fiend,
Thou false seducer of our hearts, begone!"

but don't take the school-marms, for—

"I loved Ophelia (a school-marm).
Forty thousand brothers could not
With all their quantity of love do more!"

How truly did Shenstone, who being a Shen-stone, was harder than a Brick, say—

"In every village marked with little spire,
Embowered in trees and hardly known to fame,
A matron old, whom we school-mistress name,
Who boasts unruly brats with birch to tame."

Taming is good—*tanning* would be better! We think of the past—of the little boyish days when, just for dropping a small piece of ice down the back of Mary ——, our sweetheart, so called, we took a rest across the knees of a school-marm, and—and—and it's a tender subject! We can't tell the particulars, don't ask us to, but hers was a stern duty, and all the rest of that day it seemed as if we were sitting on long sticks of pepper-candy!

Oh! generous warmth, how easy to find
A something hot behind you!
That is, if you are bound not to mind,
The indignant school-marm, mind you!"

Just then the roar of battle over the hill told of an engagement. Stonewall Jackson rode up and shouted—

"Brick" and the School-Marms.

"By thunder, ain't she handsome? Such eyes, such a kissable mouth, such a winning look, enough to make every scholar love her, and don't I wish I was a scholar that I might—

Here we are, on the school-marms again!

We can't write to-day—the spirit is willing, but the flesh is weak. There is too much excitement in the air — too much school-marm. And only think—

"Mother, I've come home to drink!"

All the school-marms are to be courted, kissed, caressed, wedded, go to housekeeping, and, in time—read this article and say if it is so or not! None of your business—if you can't guess, we won't tell. And they will all have lovers, and all be happy—

> When their spanking days are over
> And the ferule is at rest—
> When the school-marms all have husbands,
> And—well—never mind the rest

230 *"Brick" and the School-Marms.*

Pretty soon they will leave—they will rise their Convention and go somewhere, and the places that knew them will speak of them for many a day. And they will in time return to their stern duties, and the children of the State will be kept warm!

> How I'd like to be a teacher,
> And with the school-marms go,
> For here are just a few mas-cu-lines
> To a hundred girls or so!

Well, they are a good thing, and we can't have too much of them. They will excuse this chapter of nonsense, for girls always affect us in that way. We must have our say, and they'd rather we'd say this than keep silent. We love school-marms, if they are good — and most of them in this country are. We wish them well—hope they will have a pleasant visit—enjoy their trip—have a glorious ride on the river—have lots of fun—all find good lovers, and in time have lots of children for other school-marms to care for. And rather than have them come here in a body and pull our ears, or switch our walkers, we'd rather they would, when over their ramble and visit, go home and spank niggerism out of the lambs of their respective flocks, and teach the young to love the white folks and the school-marms, as well as does,

    Figuratively thine,
      "BRICK" POMEROY.

CHAPTER XXV.

WISCONSIN SCHOOL-MARM CONVENTION.

ON one of the ships that sail up and down the national ravine, from La Crosse to St. Paul, went two hundred school-marms of both sexes, all ages and conditions, marital and otherwise. The doings at La Crosse had terminated in a *Balling spell*, Basely played on the most be-nine of the teachers! The girls had been looked at and their sweethearts envied—the smart male marms had unloaded their brains—the nimphis and muggins had been filled up with ice-water and fresh air—we had looked and longed and longed and looked at this peripatetic bower of education for three days and—*Selah!*

The party had started for St. Paul. It was a motley growp. The ship was crowded, and no berths to be had for all the school-marms. The boat squeaked and creaked from stem to stern—the bed-bugs hastened hither and yon, anticipating a reach feast. The other passengers wondered why all this was all thus, and on we went like a toad after flies. Rock after rock was passed. Sloos of islands, and islands of sloos were left. We had looked here, and "do look there," and "just look over yonder," and "then see that" for six hours, until there was not an untired l—imb on any of the educational branches, when a business meeting for the purpose of developing educational points was organized.

Professor Jehiel Jagboys was chosen President, and Miss Boardie Round elected Secretary, by a majority of two.

The meeting was called to order, and "Brick" Pomeroy, an invited guest, was chosen reporter for the occasion.

Prof. Jagboys arose, steadied himself by a chair, and said—

"Gentlemen and lady school-marms! We move. Our—our—our—is onward and upwards (cheers). We move again. From point to point. We pass—pass—pass—pass—as we do points of interest on this big creek."

"Jes so, Jehiel," said the Secretary.

"We meet. We meet here. We did meet here. This is a big river. We are all on it."

"Hear—hear!" by everybody.

"That is to say. We are on the river to see it.

"Come rest on this bosom.'

And so we go home from first to last—from end to end of this matter. And now I thank you. Jehiel Jagboys thanks you. This is the first honor of the kind I ever had. We will now hear reports on education." And Jehiel doubled himself down.

Miss Squiggle, from Squiggleville, arose.

"Mr. President, I agree with you in all you have said, and more too. I have long had the same idea! It is now thirty-two years since I hung my bonnet behind the door of a schoolus, and made of that right hand a *warming-pan!* I'm goin' to tell my 'sperince! You see me now —look at me. I've grown old in this ere business, but, thank God, I've never lost my patience nor my beauty!

"There is two ways to eddicate the children of folks. There is one way, and *there* is another way, *also!* I knows it! Books ain't so much as gover'ment! Gover'ment is more as books. As for me, give me fewer books and more gover'ment.

"When bloomin' beauty hung like a topaz on my brow, I was in demand on them account. Some folks want a schoolus in the woods, so they can get gads quick. Gads is good, but give me hands—and—and—and something to warm 'em on! I never use mittens, Mr. President! There is a better way to warm hands!

"When I was examined by Mr. Warmus, he spoke of gover'ment, and I agreed with him. I had a powerful examination. All the trustees was there. I have brought a diafram of the schoolus in which I was examined, and the questions asked.

"I took off my bonnet, and we had the following dialogue:

"Deacon Warmus, Trustee—'Miss Squiggles, be you intended for a teachist?'

"Miss Squiggles, applicant—'If you please, thank you.'

"'What is your best hold?'

"'Gover'ment! always. Do you see those hand?'

"'Have you ever teachered any?'

"'Not much, but I have practised the rudiments on ten younger brats of our family!'

"'Do you understand the rule of three?'

"'I have never practised on but one at a time, but I had the other two ready!'

"'Are you familiar with the tables?'

"'I always warms 'em across my knee!'

"'What would be your favorite way to correct the bad youth of the school?'

"'I'll show you!'

"'Never mind! What salary do you want?'

"'Two dollars a month!'

"I was engaged at once. Our vicinity was noted for educational facilities, as some of the best rail-splitters in the world came from our school—their energies warmed into life by that hand, Mr. President! I wish I had a dollar, Mr. President, for every *end* that hand has *accomplished!* I'd be rich, and have a new waterfall every day, Mr. President!

"I used to enjoy teachin', till they got to makin' boys pants t'other side to! That rather busted me!

"How well I remember once when I called a boy up to receive his regular warmin'! He was the worstest boy in school. He grew up and got to editin' a paper in La Crosse; and don't I wish I had him to warm now? He was a rebel then, and allers will be!

"I got him all ready to warm, and, would you believe it, his folks had made his trowsers t'other side too! That fashion beat me completely! I never was so dumbered in my life—I couldn't punish him! And his cousin, who I was to warm, too, had the same kind of trowsers, and actually laughed at me! That was a good fashion for boys! You bet!

"I don't admire wearin' that hand out beating dust out of clothes; and I move, Mr. President, that we petition Congress to pass a law that boys' pants shall be made as they was made, for the new style is a 'fringment on our rights. I've got through and sot down, Mr. President."

Mr. Miggles—J. Theophilus Miggles, instead

of common-sense John T. Miggles—took the floor and said—

"Mr. President, and other school-marms: It is with diffidence I rise. I am but a country school-marm. I have been too devoted to education to take large schools.

"I glory in schools, and every winter I teach schools. I love it. I have tried several vocations. I have taught singing-school, trapped for musk-rats, sold essence, worked melon-patches on shares, sold brass rings and jewler trinkets to the children, as they do South to niggers; have kept an eel-weir, managed a horse, clerked at election, tended toll-gate, been pound-master, exhorted, taught Grecian painting, and filled other responsible public positions, but none gave me such pleasure as teachin' a school-house!

"Gover'ment is the great thing. But it wants genius to govern. Gads is good, but they fatigue the arm, Mr. President. Duns bloks is good, but not allers big enough. There is much that is good, but water is the best. I govern by the water plan—the studies are not so dry! I stands the scholars on their heads, and pours water down their legs. Cold water in summer—hot water in winter. I thus combine pleasure with punishment! Novel and moral idea, Mr. President. The colder the day the hotter the water. It is

"*The waterfall style!*

"Some accomplish with hands—some with gads, but water is the best!

"It warms 'em to their studies, and is not so dry! I keeps a pot on the stove and boils water on purpose.

"Gover'ment is the idea.

"It ain't the teacherin' so much as the governin'. The duties of governin' school-houses is no unarduous task. I agree with Miss Squiggles, who teaches into the next deestrict from me, that books is nothing to governin'. That pint allers bothered me. There was Jake Josling—he was the wursterest boy in all the school. I could keep track of his books better nor his tricks. It is pleasant to board around, and to visit on terms of equality with everybody.

"There was Squire Smith—he lived in fine style. His folks was so glad to have me come. They lived in a big house, and allers made it so comfortable for me. I had a bed all to myself. It was so nice.

"And at Deacon Brown's I had such a good time. The Deacon was always glad to see me. He knew I was bashful at meal-times, so he let me eat with the children, and sleep with them, too! Nothing like boarding round when you're allers welcome.

"But as I was saying, governin' a school is ticklish business. Jake Josling was the wursterest boy I ever saw. I have, as Miss Squiggles so happily said, accomplished his end often, but to no purpose! And I have gently warmed his—as I said before—with a ferule, till the object of my attention looked like a pile of rails struck by a tornado! Feruling is good, but is hard work for the arms. Pulling hair is good, but it gets grease on the fingers. Pulling ears is good, but the fingers slip off! Settin' boys and girls together is good, but it takes too much time to watch 'em. Pouring ink on their heads is very good, Mr. President, but it wastes the ink.

"And, then, it is such fun to have the confidence of your scholars; to have them put wax on your chair, red pepper in your handkerchief, oil in your inkstand, and fetta on the stove. I love playful children, Mr. President, better than I do the good boys and girls, for it gives us more chance to accomplish their ends!

"I'm in favor of governin' more and booking less. I, too, with Miss Squiggles, was once dumbfounded by the discovery I made once in regard to the new style of pants. It shocked me to see parents thus interfering to protect their childen in sin."

The convention here adjourned for lunch, and Mr. Theophilus Miggles and Miss Squiggles went arm-in-arm aft, seated themselves on a sofa, and told of school incidents; as how they had larruped children of the same fathers, warmed infants of the same mothers, and decided to mingle their destinies hereafter.

The last we saw of this brace of teachists, Squiggles was sitting on a capstan-head, while Miggles was trotting around, pushing on a capstan-bar, revolving his inamorata that she might see the country! The hot sun was beaming severely down on his uncovered knob, the sweat of perspiration exuding and trickling like limber molasses down his neck as he pantingly toiled, while the angelic Squiggles, with chin up and waterfall thrown back, was singing—

"Please, mamma—may I go and swim?"
"Yes, my dearest daughter—

If you'll hang your clothes on a hickory limb,
And not go near the water!"

Schoolmurmuringly thine,

"BRICK" POMEROY.

CHAPTER XXVI.

The Fun of Sleighing.

FUN! Of course it's *fun*, or poets would not sing, editors write, and young people dream of sleigh-riding. What every one said was so, we thought must be so, and Saturday afternoon we tried it on. First, we engaged as handsome a young lady as there is in La Crosse. Oh perplexity! but she has captured us, sure! Then we rented the use of a fast horse, dashing little conch-shell of a cutter, two buffalo-robes made out of red cloth and wolf-skins, pair of fur gloves with long wrists and soft imitation mutton-fur on the outside, a smooth hairy machine to envelop our ears in, and around we went to the snug little Gothic cottage wherein does reside the girl who went with us.

Fun! Of course we were bound to have fun! It was cold. Ice-cream in a hail-storm is no comparison. We drew up in front of the house. The horse was a fast one—dasn't tie him—spirited creature—had run away and killed two doctors a week before! We holloed. The girl came to the window. We nodded. She nodded and ran away. We waited there, shivering like a Michigan ague, our molars, cuspids, and bicuspids rattling in our head like Spanish castinets. But don't it take a girl a long time to dress? Guess not, Mary Ann! We grew tired of waiting. Horse got mad. We waited and amused ourselves with chattering "Pop goes the weasel!" In about an hour she came out. We helped her into the cutter. She was all hoops—large circumferous hoops!

The Fun of Sleighing. 247

She got in—occupied five-sixths of the seat! We crowded in edgewise like a coon-skin on a barn-door, and about as comfortable! We started for the river, rattlety-skeeter, snowballs flying and bells jingling. Somebody said it was delicious riding on the ice. We headed that way, and up stream we went, with the wind to our back, bound for fun.

Good Providence! how cold it was! A cast-iron dog in a well was nothing to it! Tried to talk! Not a bit of it! Tried to laugh at it. Froze our face all up wapsided like the price of railroad stock! She said her fingers were cold. We tried to get hold of them with one hand for the purpose of warming them. Too cold for that, even. It rode *smooth* enough, but how *alfired* cold! Toes ached? Rather think they did! And her toes, ditto! Soon her cheeks began to crack open with the frost—her lips began to chap! Had read somewhere that *two-lip* salve was good for such attacks! Thought it would be nice to apply a little! Got the horse to "whoa" slightly. We dropped the reins over the dash and our foot. She "snugged up" toward us as gently as a juvenile dove. We never had kissed her, but thought this a good time. We "whoa'd" the horse a little more—gently placed our right arm around her muffled waist, our left arm around her—her neck, low down, and she sort of leaned toward us! All this time we were going up the river at the rate of ten miles an hour. We thought she was freezing! Heard somewhere that *two-lip* salve was an "anecdote" for *that!* Had some along in case of an emergency! We got all ready—looked behind to see if any one was in sight to make remarks about us—looked ahead to see if all was clear around the bend, and then—"We-*e-e*-E-E!"—but what an *unearthly scream!* We didn't kiss her just then! Never knew it was so painful to apply the salve before! When she screamed, the horse jumped. She leaned back. One of our hands caught between her and the cutter seat. We grabbed for the reins — got them twisted and fast around left boot! Pulled with the left hand on the "gee" rein. Ran against the bank, upset the confounded conch-shell cutter, and *both of us got out!*—"Y-y-yip"— how easy! The way we go out might have been graceful there, but it would not have been in Broadway. It might have been elegant, but we doubt it! It might have been deliberate— only it wasn't! We got out of the cutter, however, *quick as it upset!* Being more polite, we got out first! Then came the young lady, with another "We-e-*e*-*e*-E-E!" only a little shorter! She lit on our head. Her garments were not draped, nor did they appear in festoons. We were under, the good Lord only knows how many yards of mixed goods! We crawled out and beheld a general assortment of thick-soled shoes, white woollen hose, red elastics, skirts, skeleton thing, furs, shawls, merino, and young lady, sadly and badly mixed! The horse had gone home with the cutter, robes, and one boot pulled off by the reins! We were nine miles from home! We helped the girl up and smoothed down her raiment. She was mad. Says she, "I'll tell my ma!" Says we, "Don't!" Says she, "You mean feller — upset a-purpose!" We denied the *soft* impeachment, but it was no use, and we started home on foot. Well, if it *wan't* chilly! How our teeth chattered! Our noses looked as blue as an old cent! She was mad! Ditto. She said sleighing was a humbug! Ditto. She said she'd never go out with a "Brick" again! We walked half a mile. The sleet was driving in our face awfully. Looked back, and saw, two miles off, a team coming. Sat down on the ice to rest. Bundled up the girl—took off our Russian coat, sat down by her on the ice to keep her warm. It was rather cool where we sat! Moved a little—didn't feel it as much. Her cheeks looked inflamed. Our heart felt the same way! She sighed, and we sided up to her. Told her two-lip salve *was* good. She didn't doubt it, but it was too cold to spread well! We tried it again. We-e-*e-e*-E-E! It must have been the *cold* that made it hurt so to apply the salve. In-doors, it's fun to use it. We sat there and waited. The team hove in sight! Drove up and stopped. It was a Norwegian with a load of wood! Good rugged place for young lady to ride, but there was no help. She got up. We tried to, and couldn't. Pants had froze fast to the ice! Tried again—"rip!" and how the cold air rushed in upon our spinal membrino! Tried again, and "rip," and more cold air. The girl took us by the hand—another "rip!" and a piece of our French doeskin pants, about the size of the end of a muff, lay there on the cold ice! We complained of the cold. Norwegian said it would be warmer, if we wore drawers. Agreed with him! Helped the young lady climb on the sled—bundled her up with overcoat and light wood, and came along very gradually, indeed. Asked Norwegian his name. He said it was Turner Overson! Young lady heard the last sentence—thought he meant it—jumped off with another "We-e-*e-e*-E-E!—no you don't!" She wouldn't ride there are any more! Hired a sleigh and driver, and enveloped in cold straw and shivers, and came into the city behind two mules, at the rate of a mile in two hours. Half a mile to each mule! We took the young lady home, and have not been to see her since. The doctor says her nose, one ear, both cheeks, one hand, and one foot are frost-bitten! We are worse off than that. Haven't been out of the house for a week back! We're all frosted, from top to toe.

The Fun of Sleighing.

The horse came home in speed and disgust. He spilt the robes, broke the cutter, and sprained his leg, so we have him to pay for. Our ride—our immensely pleasant ride, has cost us over four hundred dollars already, besides the loss of a kiss, the young lady, and a few thousands after marriage! If we ever go out for such fun, some blind man will please shoot us. If that is sport, we pass! It's a humbug—a chimera—a delusion—a—a—a horn-swogglement. We shall never engage in it again. If you want to sleigh-ride, go it, but excuse us. This freezing to death for the sake of sitting by the side of a pretty girl, is all a humbug, especially when Sunday nights are as long as now.

P. S.—A pair of fur gloves, hair thing for the ears, and muffler, for sale cheap. They are fine articles, but the owner has no further use for them!

CHAPTER XXVII.

SLOBBERING PARTIES—FOR THE HEATHEN!

A MODEST rap, rap and a half, or two raps on the door.

"Come in."

"Good-morning, 'Brick.'"

"Ditto, Deacon."

"To-night we have a sociable at our house—a meeting of those who are willing to do a little something for the benefit of the heathen—a social gathering of young and old, and we wish you to attend."

"What's the exercise programme?"

"Oh! nothing out of the way—social sociability—chat with the ladies—promenade with the girls—games—reading from a book—a little fun—contribution—refreshments, such as cold water and opening and closing the draft to the stove!—good-night—home with the girls, etc."

"Will attend!"

"And bring a lady?"

"And bring a lady'"

"Good-morning!"

"Ditto, Deacon!"

After supper we read Chesterfield. Then we looked through our wardrobe for a ruffled shirt. Then we gave a barber ten cents for a dime's worth of facing. The next move was to eradicate the dust from our imported goods. This done, with trembling heart we started for the soci.

We always were some on the ambition. Actuated thus, we had invited the handsomest girl in La Crosse to go with us to help the heathen out of their religious panic. She was *the* flower of the family, and there were thirteen flowers of them! She was handsome—dreadfully hans. She was the sweetest in the rosary—the gayest of the gay—the one *altogether* lovely. When we emerged outside from the sill of her father's domicile, and saw Bluffer, our rival, riding by with a mad look, how our heart ambitionated as she placed her pretty hand within the graceful bend of our broadcloth! Guess not.'

We went to the sociable.

Everybody was there. The house was crowded. Didn't know the heathen had so many friends. Our Mirilda—that's her name—was the prettiest girl there. That made us feel good. We were late, and the chairs, sofas, settees, ottomans, stools, etc., were occupied. Mirilda must have a seat, and to get it she had to sit on the wood-box. Didn't like that. We stood up. The sociable began. A nasal chap read something—couldn't tell what. Then commenced the chat with the ladies. Mirilda was the rose every one was after. Good for Mirilda, but we didn't relish it. Every putty-head in the room was bound to monopolize her. We felt mad, and inwardly said, darn the heathen. Then we had games. There were forfeits to pay, and old Mother Wattles was the judge. She did not like us, because we did not marry *her* daughter. She knew we hankered after Mirilda, because we had told her in confidence, and, unable to hold so important an item alone, she had got the help of all the old gossips in the city. She was judge, as before stated, and every time a feller did anything she made him kiss Mirilda.

DARN THE HEATHEN.

Deacon Rattler did something, and he must make a "butter bowl" with our own sweet girl. And he put his hands over his ugly face, and blindfold kissed her six several and distinct times; right in the mouth at that! The gray old nuisance! To see him kissing Mirilda made us feel as a lady feels to see a jackass stamping around in a bed of pinks.

Then a little runt with some goose-fuzz on his upper lip had to kiss her ten times. Then the school-master had to take a trial at it, with his essence-of-cinnamon-scented head! Then a dozen dry-goods clerks, who Mirilda never would have let kiss her if it wasn't for fashion, had to help themselves to bliss from her ruby warehouse!

DARN THE HEATHEN.

After a while—a very long while, too, it came our turn, and we stood *madus erectus in frontis* the plethoric female judiciary! We knew she would tell us to kiss Mirilda, and we decided not to do it—just out of spite! But confound her if she didn't sentence us to go and get down on our knees before Miss Slimmer, an old maid of fifty-five, and then she was to kneel too, and we were to kiss her twelve times by the thermometer! We did it! Miss Slimmer went at it like a dog after a rabbit, but then we do wish she'd let onions alone till *after* such exercises.

They don't add to such things, even in her case!

CONFOUND THE HEATHEN.

At last the sociable was over! Our Mirilda had been kissed, slobbered, mussed, and mousled over by every chap in the room till she looked like a pan of currants, half green, half ripe! The plate was passed, and each donated. Not a donate from us! *We passed, too!* We felt dreadfully womblecropt, and with Mirilda on our arm went home, disgusted with all such "kissing bees" for the sake of the heathen—confound them! We didn't stay long at her house. We felt mad like! Mirilda felt sort of poorly, too, and said she didn't want to go again. Said she'd rather buy those groceries by the retail, as too many of them spoiled the market! We kissed her good-night, and from her lips we tasted cardamom seeds, tobacco, cloves, sardines, cassia buds, lager-beer, camomile flowers, Switzer cheese, gin cocktails, liquorice root, hard cider, sweet flag, and the Lord only knows what else! All the effects of promiscuous kissing—for the benefit of the heathen!

Fashion sanctions it? Darn fashion! That's all! Who wants to take the girl he loves to such parties, where every mutton-head has license to kiss, slobber, and mousel over lips which at no other time could he dare to touch! It must be pleasant for girls to be chawed up and slobbered over by everybody in the room. It's so modest! It looks so angelic-like! When woman's lips become public property, we quit. How sweet is the kiss tinctured up like a drug store! It looks so retiring and lady-like to see a pair of ruby lips one has a love for, sitting out like a horse block! Fashion may tolerate it, but fashion is a fool—a very foolish fool at that! It will do to *steal* kisses by moonlight—when sleigh-riding—when standing by the gate to say good-night; or to delicately pluck those ripe enough to fall, as you sit on a sofa with the lamp turned down as if asleep, one arm around the waist, the head carelessly resting on your shoulder, and the lips just opened as heaven opens to let in a loved spirit; but this promiscuous slobbering, with a hundred raw eyes watching and waiting for a like chance, is too much for the human.

CONFOUND YOUR HEATHEN-*ish* PARTIES!

CHAPTER XXVIII.

WONDERFUL HAIR-REPRODUCER.

DR. ———, of New York, sent us a cake of his Onguent, with the modest request to "puff it, and send the bill." Venerable and far-sighted capillary producer! We do, and more too. Your Onguent is a big thing. Although in small cakes, it is nevertheless a colossal item. We tried it. Following the printed directions given, we made a lather and applied the brush. The lather was mixed in a glass dish, and in four minutes a beautiful hair, all shades of color, had started from the dish. We applied some to our face, and it took four swift-working barbers to cut down and mow away as fast as the beard grew. We put a little on the toe of each boot, and in an hour they looked like Zouave mustaches. We put some on a crowbar, and it is covered with long, curly hair like a buffalo, and in the coldest weather it can be used without mittens. A little on the carriage-pole started the hair on it like moss. We dropped some on the stove, and as the fire was kindled the hair started, and the hotter the stove became, the faster grew the hair, till the smell of the burnt hair became so powerful as to drive all from the room. The stove was set in the barn, and it can't be seen now, as the hair is literally stacked upon it. Only one application. A little applied on a wagon-tire has in five days started a vigorous crop, and now the wagon can be driven over a plank-road and not make the least noise, so well are the wheels covered with soft hair. Only one application—

dollar a cake. We skinned a goose, put on some of the Onguent, and in two hours the feather-grower was enveloped in hair like a squirrel, and was seen this morning trying to climb a shagbark hickory in the back-yard. A little applied to the inkstand has given it a coat of bristles, making a splendid pen-wiper at little cost. We applied the lather to a tenpenny nail, and the nail is now the handsomest lather-brush you ever saw, with a beautiful growth of soft hair at the end of it, some five or six feet in length. Only a dollar a cake! Applied to door stones, it does away with the use of a mat. Applied to a floor, it will cause to grow therefrom hair sufficient for a Brussels carpet. A little of this Onguent lather was accidentally dropped on the head of our cane, which has been perfectly bald for over ten years, and immediately a thick growth of hair formed, completely covering it, compelling us to shave the head twice a week. Only a dollar a bottle—directions thrown in. A little weak

Wonderful Hair-Reproducer. 265

lather sprinkled over a barn makes it impervious to wind, rain, or cold. It is good to put inside of children's cradles—sprinkle on sidewalks, anything, where luxuriant grass is wanted for use or ornament. We put a little on the head of navigation, and a beautiful hair covered it. A little on the mouth of Mississippi river started hair there resembling the finest red-top grass, in which cows, sheep, pigs, hogs, snipes, woodcock, and young ducks graze with keen relish. Only a dollar a cake. Sent by mail to any address. One application will grow a luxuriant mustache for a boy. One dollar a cake. Samson used it.

CHAPTER XXIX.

The Dickens.

BOZ.

We saw him.

'E came from Hengland! Came hover the hocean hin two steamers, the blarsted things! He came over to collect interest on his notes of Americans taken some years since. He said the Americans were hall Hasses, and——the Dickens!

The Lord loveth whom he chasteneth.

We all love whomsoever chastiseth us. Selah.

Therefore, the Dickens.

We did saw him!

Great men are always fashionable. The folks

turn out to welcome great men and those they love. They rushed to see Lincoln's funeral. They paid to see the late prize-fight. They welcomed the Portland gag Weston, the walkist, whose pleasant fictions as to wagers, and so forth, reminds us of Dickens.

The papers have told all they know about WESTON. Some of them have had special correspondents to tell us of Dickens—who he was, how he was, what he was, when he was, where he was, why he was, which he was, and how he acted while he was!

The New York papers are not particular enough. Their readers are great for gossip and raising the Dickens. We pattern after New York papers and cater only to those who follow lions and flutter like tails to foreign kites.

Dickens came.

Then he came again.

This is his second coming.

We saw him land. We sat on the top of

Bunker Hill Monument and saw him come ashore. We ran ahead of him to New York and saw him there. He came in by Communipaw, Murray Street, the Central Park, Tammany Hall, Mozart Wood pile, and down the Broadway!

He is—the Dickens.

He was dressed in men's clothes—or one man's clothes at all events. They were made in England. He had hair on his head, and what he could not put there he had on his face. He wore a coat, and a penknife. He walked in from the Hub for his constitutional. He emulates Weston, only Weston beat the Dickens. He entered the hotel by the front door. He walked very fast—made the distance, eight miles from the carriage to the hotel door, inside his—under shirt!

His boots were worn on his feet, while he wore his hat on his head! He sells enough waste paper each day to buy a rose for his button-hole. The paper comes from those who wish him t(

exhibit himself at their houses. This would make the next door and the other set of fellows feel bad! The Dickens!

He eateth not of mustard. So does a cat! Very unfeline not to eat mustard! He eats mutton chops and pulls wool. Selah!

He has two agents and nine body-servants. And many servants for his legs! He says come here, and they goeth—and go there, and they cometh!

He uses a fork. He makes 'em all fork over! We saw him arise once. It was in the morning —before breakfast. This is the how of it.

At half-past three o'clock A. M. he turned over and squeaked the bed to see if his agent had come in. Then he sneezed out of one nose. Then he sneezed out of the other. Then he sneezed out of both at once. Three times. He then pulled the top sheet over his right eyebrow, turned to his left wing, and slept like a babe taking its catnip or kit nap!

At four he slung the sheet from his chin, turned over again and gently put his left foot out of bed. One of his leg servants then drew on his hose. He dresses the left foot first. This is not right, for he eats no mustard. So does a cat!

Then his garments were wafted on him, all but the rose in his button-hole. He washed his face in the basin. Used water, wet his hands before he did his face. This is peculiarly English. Then he combed his hair by proxy, and while one of his servants was cleaning his teeth, wrote a ten-thousand-dollar article for the Mamby Pamby *Pass Book*.

At six o'clock he sneezed again. It was the mustard!

At seven he tasted a glass of water, and at eight poked his head out of the window to hear an Italian boy from Dublin sing, as he trudged along between two tin pails—

Clams to sell! Fine clams to day!
Clams nice and soft from Rockaway!

The Dickens.

> Clams to bake and clams to fry,
> And clams to make a clam pot-pie
> Oh Clams!
> Oh Clams!
> Soft clams!
> Tell your dads and tell your mams
> That I'm the boy to sell 'em clams!

This little testimonial will be printed in volume two of his American Notes, price ten pence ha'penny!

At nine he breakfasted. He entered the dining-room by deploying from the left, striking the table in an oblique position on the extreme centre. He then caromed on a soft-boiled potato, levied on a link of fried eel, pulled an eye-winker from his left eye, camped on a hot buckwheat pancake rather syruptitiously, drove his picket into a country sausage, illustrated an edition of porter-house beef-steak with cuts, made a water-fall of a glass of milk, wrestled with it two inches higher than his cheek bone, and downed a piece of butter and sneezed gently at the mustard!

Dickens uses tea. He uses it for a beverage. He holds the cup even with his cheek bone, in his left hand, and dips it in with a teaspoon. He refused to allow Butler to call on him during tea-time!

At ten o'clock he shoves the table from him and sits down against the wall to write. He is quite a noted writer. He writes for fun while waiting for something to turn up. Then he looks over his tickets, gives the counterfeit ones to dead heads, writes a letter to his publishers, and tries the hall for its acoustic properties. When he walks he puts one leg before the other. The faster he walks the faster he moves his legs. But he uses no mustard!

He is commanding—orders a gin-cocktail whenever he wants one, except in Boston!

When writing he sits in a chair if convenient, places the paper before him, takes the pen in his right hand, dips it occasionally in an inkstand and winks. He always winks as he dips his pen, but uses no mustard!

He is the author of several works, in which respect he resembles Brigham Young more than George Washington, who used mustard!

He telegraphed into Boston from mid-ocean that he was sea-sick, and should leave the steamer and walk in, so an extra boat was sent out to meet him. One day when dining with Deacon Brown, of the Two-hundredth-street Church, he got off a joke which startled the Brown family.

Said Mrs. Deacon Brown—

"My dear Mr. Dickens, how did you like the sea on your trip?"

Said Charles—

"I see too much of it—let us wave the subject! *O shun* it, I pray!"

The Browns all laughed immoderately. But

Dickens would not eat their mustard! Then Mrs. Deacon Brown asked if he was sea-sick.

Then Mr. Dickens responded—

"You bet! Every man of sense is sea-sick. So was I. I was disgusted, and I thought of the person who attempted a sea voyage on the sea of Galilee, was sea-sick, disgusted, and got out and walked!"

Deacon Brown looked at his wife, but neither of them smiled. It was the mustard!

In person Mr. Dickens resembles his pictures quite much, but the resemblance is not so striking as it was. Mr. Dickens brought a few intimate friends with him to this country, the society here being so poor, and it is now his intention to visit a few of the wealthy but honest families of New York and Boston with his select party, for the purpose of giving us Americans lessons in manners, politeness, and civilization without *mustard!*

NEW BOOKS
And New Editions Recently Published by
CARLETON, Publisher,
NEW YORK.

N.B.—THE PUBLISHER, upon receipt of the price in advance, will send any of the following Books by mail, POSTAGE FREE, to any part of the United States. This convenient and very safe mode may be adopted when the neighboring Booksellers are not supplied with the desired work. State name and address in full.

Victor Hugo.

LES MISÉRABLES.—The celebrated novel. One large 8vo volume, paper covers, $2.00 ; . . . cloth bound, $2.50
LES MISÉRABLES.—In the Spanish language. Fine 8vo. edition, two vols., paper covers, $4.00 ; . . cloth bound, $5.00
JARGAL.—A new novel. Illustrated. . 12mo. cloth, $1.75
CLAUDE GUEUX, and Last Day of Condemned Man. do. $1.50

Miss Muloch.

JOHN HALIFAX.—A novel. With illustration. 12mo. cloth, $1.75
A LIFE FOR A LIFE.— , do. do. $1.75

Charlotte Bronte (Currer Bell).

JANE EYRE.—A novel. With illustration. 12mo. cloth, $1.75
THE PROFESSOR.— do. . do. . do. $1.75
SHIRLEY.— . do. . do. . do. $1.75
VILLETTE.— . do. . do. . do. $1.75

Hand-Books of Society.

THE HABITS OF GOOD SOCIETY; with thoughts, hints, and anecdotes, concerning nice points of taste, good manners, and the art of making oneself agreeable. The most entertaining work of the kind. . . . 12mo. cloth, $1.75
THE ART OF CONVERSATION.—With directions for self-culture. A sensible and instructive work, that ought to be in the hands of every one who wishes to be either an agreeable talker or listener. . . . . 12mo. cloth, $1.50
ARTS OF WRITING, READING, AND SPEAKING.—An excellent book for self-instruction and improvement . . 12mo. cloth, $1.50
HAND-BOOKS OF SOCIETY.—The above three choice volumes are also bound in extra style, full gilt ornamental back, uniform in appearance, and put up in a handsome box. Price for the set of three, ... $5.00

Algernon Charles Swinburne.

LAUS VENERIS, AND OTHER POEMS.— . 12mo, cloth, $1.75

Mrs. Mary J. Holmes' Works.

LENA RIVERS.—	A novel.	12mo. cloth,	$1.50
DARKNESS AND DAYLIGHT.—	do.	do.	$1.50
TEMPEST AND SUNSHINE.—	do.	do.	$1.50
MARIAN GREY.—	do.	do.	$1.50
MEADOW BROOK.—	do.	do.	$1.50
ENGLISH ORPHANS.—	do.	do.	$1.50
DORA DEANE.—	do.	do.	$1.50
COUSIN MAUDE.—	do.	do.	$1.50
HOMESTEAD ON THE HILLSIDE.—	do.	do.	$1.50
HUGH WORTHINGTON.—	do.	do.	$1.50
THE CAMERON PRIDE.—	do.	do.	$1.50
ROSE MATHER.—	do.	do.	$1.50
ETHELYN'S MISTAKE.—*Just Published.*	do.	do.	$1.50

Miss Augusta J. Evans.

BEULAH.—A novel of great power.		12mo. cloth,	$1.75
MACARIA.— do.	do.	do.	$1.75
ST. ELMO.— do.	do. *Just Published.*	do.	$2.00

By the Author of "Rutledge."

RUTLEDGE.—A deeply interesting novel.		12mo. cloth,	$1.75
THE SUTHERLANDS.—	do.	do.	$1.75
FRANK WARRINGTON.—	do.	do.	$1.75
ST. PHILIP'S.—	do.	do.	$1.75
LOUIE'S LAST TERM AT ST. MARY'S.—		do.	$1.75
ROUNDHEARTS AND OTHER STORIES.—For children.	do.		$1.75
A ROSARY FOR LENT.—Devotional Readings.		do.	$1.75

Captain Mayne Reid's Works—Illustrated.

THE SCALP HUNTERS.—	A romance.	12mo. cloth,	$1.75
THE RIFLE RANGERS.—	do.	do.	$1.75
THE TIGER HUNTER.—	do.	do.	$1.75
OSCEOLA, THE SEMINOLE.—	do.	do.	$1.75
THE WAR TRAIL.—	do.	do.	$1.75
THE HUNTER'S FEAST.—	do.	do.	$1.75
RANGERS AND REGULATORS.—	do.	do.	$1.75
THE WHITE CHIEF.—	do.	do.	$1.75
THE QUADROON.—	do.	do.	$1.75
THE WILD HUNTRESS.—	do.	do.	$1.75
THE WOOD RANGERS.—	do.	do.	$1.75
WILD LIFE.—	do.	do.	$1.75
THE MAROON.—	do.	do.	$1.75
LOST LEONORE.—	do.	do.	$1.75
THE HEADLESS HORSEMAN.—	do.	do.	$1.75
THE WHITE GAUNTLET.—*Just Published.*		do.	$1.75

Printed in Dunstable, United Kingdom